In Search of Gold

John Fisk
(As pictured in later life in F. C. Pierce's 1896 Fisk genealogy)

In Search of Gold

Journal of Incidents on Land and Sea

John Fisk

Edited by Bruce Adam

Ara Pacis

In Search of Gold
Journal of Incidents on Land and Sea
By John Fisk;
Edited by Bruce Adam

Copyright © 2005 by Bruce Ormsby Adam.

All rights reserved. Printed in the United States of America. No part of this book may be used or reproduced in any manner whatsoever without written permission except in the case of brief quotations embodied in critical articles and reviews.

First Paperback Edition, 2005

Ara Pacis Publishers
P.O. Box 1202
Des Plaines, IL 60017-1202
www.arapacispublishers.com

ISBN 0-9661318-3-5
Library of Congress Control Number: 2004112671
Manufactured in the United States of America

Preface

It has been one hundred years since John Fisk died, but without this wonderful journal that he kept of his experiences, there isn't much we would know about him. Here are most of the facts that anyone could ascertain regarding his life: He is listed in Frederick C. Pierce's *Fiske and Fisk Family*, a genealogy published in 1896 with noticeable inaccuracies, as having been born in Lexington, Massachusetts on November 6, 1827, though from his own account and the dates on his gravestone, he was actually born in 1829. The genealogy also omits one of his forefathers. I've included a short appendix at the end of this volume to clarify this. On March 13, 1856 he married Judith Decrow, of Lincolnville, ME and lived with her in Billerica, MA where they had six children. We also know from the genealogy that his father Jonathan, a shoemaker and farmer born in 1786 in Lexington, lived during the latter part of his life with his son John in Billerica until he died there in 1871.

John Fisk is also listed in the 1905 Billerica, MA Directories as a farmer living on Manning Rd. at the corner of Old Middlesex Tpk. In 1905 his daughter, Miss Augusta Fisk, is listed as living with him as a boarder, and Merton Fisk (his son) is listed as a poulterer living on Wyman Rd. near the Bedford line. The 1911 Directory (the first one available after the 1905) has Miss Augusta as the boarder of Mrs. J. Fisk; Judith Fisk is listed as the widow of John W. Fisk (who died Feb. 12, 1905) and living on Boston Rd, near Charnstaffe Ln. In this Directory, Merton is listed as then living in the Manning Rd. property. The Property Valuation book for 1900 lists John Fisk as owning a dwelling house, a second small house, barn, poultry house, one horse, one cow, 20 fowl, one carriage and a homestead of 112 acres. This same book has Merton Fisk owning a dwelling house, barn, poultry houses, water works, one horse, one cow, 400 fowl and a homestead of 12 acres. Merton's first listing is in the 1900 book. John's property is listed back to 1860, with a few additions/subtractions. The Fisks' daughter Augusta died in 1948 and is buried next to her parents.

Hearing only these facts, there is really nothing compelling that would make us desire to know more, and at the same time, it is sad to consider that after several generations, less is known for most others. But the genealogy does state the following of John Fisk: "He was one of the California pioneers in 1849, going around Cape Horn — a six months' passage. He returned in 1850 and started again from Wilmington, sixty miles west of Chicago, Ill., with a train of three wagons, across the great plains — a six months' tramp. He returned in 1855 and settled in Billerica on his place which he has named *Elmore*, from the fact that a group of four large American elms overshadow a beautiful lawn. The youngest tree was planted the same year as the erection of the house, in 1796."

To my mind, it is strange to find such a statement of adventure woven within such mundane information, except that when John Fisk finally returned to Massachusetts he seemed committed to losing himself in the world and his work in an affirmative and productive way as if remembering his adventures was just a part of the greater calling of living his life. He makes this clear in the last sentence of the journal. There is no mention of how much money Fisk made from gold mining. His homestead in Billerica seems to have been considerable, but there are moments in the journal where he is obviously none too prosperous. I do know from family history, as John Fisk was my great-great grandfather, that he was a cranberry farmer for about fifty years. A published poem called *The Cranberry Webb Worm* appeared at the end of his journal, and I've included it as well at the end of this volume.

Fisk kept a journal of his experiences and published it as a serial in a New England newspaper. He clipped it into a binder, and it was passed down as a kind of family treasure. I first read it in 1971 during weekends visits from Cambridge to my grandmother

Preface

(Winifred Court) in Stoneham, MA. Her sister Florence, a retired English teacher, was its guardian, and she would bring it over while I was there, but she would always take it back before I left. I asked for a copy, and before Florence died, she had copies made for distribution to the grandchildren. Winifred and Florence were John Fisk's granddaughters.

So here are some facts that we can ascertain from the journal: more than one hundred and fifty years ago, a nineteen-year-old boy named John Fisk signed on for a voyage to San Francisco. The journey took him from Boston around Cape Horn, and his party was among the first to arrive in California for the gold rush of 1849. Later, after he'd returned via Panama to Boston, he returned to San Francisco once again, only this time he set out from Illinois by wagon train after a discouraging attempt to settle there. He kept a record of all of his experiences in the journal you are about to read. But these facts, like those from the library archives and the genealogy, lack spirit, but thankfully, the gold we find in the journal emanates from the spirit of John Fisk captured in its pages. So much of what we know of the American West comes out of legend and fabrication. Documentaries that cover the era are filled with quaint quotes and snapshots that give us some sense of the times, but only at a safe distance. But the coverage of Fisk's journal from start to finish comes from one man's perspective, putting us in mind of how we might think if we'd lived in those times, and it is a far greater ride to be transported there in the words of John Fisk than by modern documentaries covering the subject. John Fisk didn't know the archetypes of his time, nor was he prone to romanticize his own era as we now tend to do. There's nothing quaint about this book.

But what can we really say we know about the times when it is impossible for us to identify with such a world? Would anyone in our time be willing to undertake a journey on a boat that would last more than five months and put us in a dangerous place thousands of miles from home? No matter how far we've come since then, it is hard to imagine going as far from where we are now in just a century and a half. Fisk accepted his era in the same way, which is why it was not a problem for him to get on the boat. On the other hand,

In Search of Gold

we think we live in such a different world until we read Fisk's account of what it cost to live as a miner. Merchants raised prices for supplies, and meals in San Francisco during the gold rush could get expensive even by our standards.

Taken for its historical information, the story is profoundly interesting in what it reveals of the way of life in the middle of nineteenth century America. No Hollywood hand shaped the text of the story, but at times it tends to read like an adventure that jumped off the screen. Take Jim's frying pan, for example. He swings it around in preference to any other weapon. This seems right out of a movie, but it came long before motion pictures. Being a pioneer was not so drab and sullen as modern documentaries might make us think.

We also get a glimpse of the character of the prejudice of the time. We grimace to see white men taking Indian scalps. Death is so common that it almost becomes a character in the story. Whether the journey to California is too much, or it's an Indian attack, or miners fighting over gold, John Fisk encountered death daily in some chapters, and his acceptance of it comes across as psychologically fitting for that time though we tend to think life didn't have to be so harsh. As for wildlife, whether it was buffalo, deer or the grizzly bear, true to most accounts, Fisk's journal shows how these animals were often killed just for fun. There are descriptions of the endless flocks of passenger pigeons, now extinct, and herds of buffalo as far as one could see. The virgin forests of the 1850s were as vast then as they are sparse today. There's interest in what this story reveals of the effect man can have in a just a few years in any era— the grinding wheel of the nineteenth century has churned through the twentieth, and now in the twenty-first, it still has momentum. We've become environmentally nostalgic now that the American wilderness is gone, but as I look back to my own childhood in the late 1950s and early 1960s, I recall in autumn how everyone was drawn outside in late autumn by the thousands of birds migrating south for the winter. My children will never see such a thing.

On another level, this is a great adventure story. The idea of riding a ship around Cape Horn to San Francisco to search for gold, and of traveling west along the route used by thousands over plains and through the mountain passes, is in the bones of every American. The opening of the West was such an exciting era, it's no wonder that it became a focus of Hollywood in so many movies. But the true flavor of the times is missing in those films. John Fisk left this personal history and marked the trail through various states that historians discuss but can't bring back to life, and he captures it in his account both in his mindset and his experiences. Many of the common sights for pioneers, the landmarks he describes, as well as the trails, such as Chimney Rock, are still out there, just off the highways heading west, hidden places worth a visit for those who might be interested. Not far from the highways, grown over with weeds, uninteresting except to the curious tourist as a brief diversion, the era lives again in these pages like towns along the Mississippi in *Huckleberry Finn*. My great-great-grandfather lives again as well as we feel that John Fisk was happy and young, that life was good despite all the dust. An eternally young and energetic John Fisk is so vividly captured that we feel we know him as a young man, and it is hard to imagine that he grew old and died a century ago.

During a recent visit to San Francisco, I thought how only four hours made up the entire journey from Chicago. There was no beef jerky on the plane, no panthers at the airport, no Indians fighting — only a city football team to stand as an immediate, empirical reminder that there really ever was a gold rush. I made the round-trip in less time than it took John Fisk to travel a dozen miles across Missouri. It was all hard work and danger back then, but thanks to those who blazed the trails we all can sit back a while and watch the San Francisco '49ers. That's how different our world has become, but the city also changed enormously between the day John Fisk arrived and the day he left. The gold rush had a profound impact.

Because the tale has value to history, I felt it was time to reprint the story as close to the original as possible, so except for a very few minor rearrangements of text, the work stands as it did when originally published. Written before the Civil War, this book includes references to slavery, a very sensitive subject, the impact of which I have softened in several instances without compromising literary or historical accuracy. Some small errors such as spelling have been

In Search of Gold

corrected to improve the flow. I've inserted brief comments or corrections in brackets in the text wherever necessary. Also, I left some errors intact with my brackets to maintain the overall authenticity of the language. I corrected the spelling of "pully" to "pulley," for example, and left "Otterway" for "Ottawa" intact, because the latter probably indicates the pronunciation of the time. I've indicated an inaccuracy or two of the route he described that did not jibe with geography. Fisk also split many compound words such as "sailfish." I left these alone as well. Occasionally I encountered an obliterated word and did my best to work around it. Improvements may yet be possible since the original manuscript in Fisk's own hand survives, but the cousin in whom it was entrusted sees fit to keep it buried in family archives. Hopefully it will find its way to the light of day so that a proper text comparison can be made. Still, except for very light editing, this version of Fisk's journal is presented not only as it was originally published, but with many improvements including a map, a detailed genealogy of Fisk's ancestry, and many pictures including one of Fisk as a young man taken shortly after he completed the adventures recounted in this volume.

In 1889, *The Associated California Pioneers of '49* was formed in Boston. John Fisk was an honored member of the society, and he received quite a large certificate in 1896 that was also passed down through the family to me. The cover artwork as well as most illustrations in the book are all from this unique document, and I hope that including them makes for a more enjoyable experience reading this story. The illustration on page 152 is of Revere House where the society kept its headquarters.

Finally, I'd like to express my thanks to Bruce Williams for his excellent and extensive genealogical work, to Fisk's grandson Richard Greene for his generosity and photographic memory, to Don Cooper of the Oregon-California Trails Association for kind help in explaining the various routes taken to California, and to the Billerica Public Library, especially Kathy Meagher, for her assistance in researching the history of John Fisk and his family there.

Bruce O. Adam

Table of Contents

Chapter I 3
The Company — The Ship New Jersey and Her Outfit — The Start — Services on Board Ship — Killing Time with Ruta Bagas — Porpoises and Flying Fish — Dividing the Company into Messes — Shirking Duty — Duff and Soft Tack — The French Cook — "Man Overboard!" — Trade Winds — River La Plate — The Storm — Brazilian Fishermen — Staten Land — Preparations to "Round the Horn" — The Falklands and Tierra del Fuego — A Ruse, "Sail ho!" — In the Pacific — "Crossing the Line" — "Old Neptune" — A Terrible Storm — In Callao — A Visit to Lima, Peru — On Board Again — Arrival at the "Golden Gate" — In San Francisco — Start for the Mines — Etc., Etc., Etc.

Chapter II 13
The Sacramento River — Wild Animals — Wild Fowl — Start for Weaver's Creek — Hotel Comforts! — "Prospecting" — The Poisoned Spring — Sickness in Camp — The Funeral — A Queer Bedfellow — The "Mysterious Rider" — Return to the States — On the Isthmus — Etc., Etc., Etc.

Chapter III 21
Down the Chagres River — Stop at Havana — Cholera on Board Ship — Arrival at New York — "Home Again" — A New Start — Going West — Among Sharpers — On the Canal — Rochester — Cleveland — Chicago — Farming on the Prairie — Corn Planting — Building a House — Wild Pigeons — Etc., Etc., Etc.

Chapter IV 30
Stray Cattle — Fear and Ague — Prairie Fires — The Corn Harvest — A Blizzard — Start Again for California — Crossing Prairie — A Rich Grain Country — Camping Out — Fellow Travellers — Starved Rock — Loss of One of the Party — A Terrible Hail Storm — Crossing a River — The Patent Grist Mill — Blacks at Work — The Amazon and her Turkeys — The Panther — Attacked by a Cougar — Etc., Etc., Etc.

Chapter V 40
Still on the March — Platte River — Small Pox — Cholera — Missouri — A Fire — Hunting and Fishing — Camp on the Missouri — Among the Arapahoes — More Trouble with the Indians — Setting Guard — Fighting the Indians — The Dead and Wounded — Crossing the Little and Big Vermillion — Arrival on the Elk-Horn River — Fish and Game — A Prairie Dog Town — A Lonely Traveller — Etc., Etc., Etc.

Chapter VI 48
The Packer — The Tornado — Attack by Indians — The Pursuit — The Fight — The Rescue — The Killed and Wounded — Return to Camp — Fort Kearney — In the Pawnee Country — The Storm — Buffalo Antelope, and Deer — The Old Bull — Crossing the South Fork of the Platte — Arrival at a Trading Post — French Canadians — The Sioux Natives — Crossing the "Glorious Fourth" — Etc., Etc., Etc.

Chapter VII..56
A New Surprise — The Wedding — The Ball — "Miss Big Wolf" — Court House Rock — Chimney Rock — Castle Rock — Crossing the North Fork of the Platte — Independence Rock — The Sweet Water — The Devil's Gate—Pacific Springs — A Hail Storm — Attacked by Wolves — A Sad Accident — Green River — Parting Company — Salt Lake Mountain — A Raid on the Cattle — The Fight — "Old Burr" Again — A Prisoner — The Punishment — Etc., Etc., Etc.

Chapter VIII 65
The City of the Mormons — Grasshoppers — Cattle, Horses and Sheep — A Mormon Interviewed — Brigham as a Preacher — The Valley — Bear River — Arrive at the Spring — A Fight with Indians — The Wounded and Slain — The Humboldt River — Etc., Etc., Etc.

Chapter IX 72
A Surprise — Jim and his Frying Pan — Arrive at the Humboldt — The "Diggers" — In Search of the Cattle — Attacked by a Digger — The Applegate Trail — Hard Travelling — The Boiling Spring — "Rabbit Hole Spring" — The Salt Plain — "Black Rock Boiling Springs" — Loss of Cattle — "Smoke Creek Canyon" — "Summer Valley" — The Sierra Nevada Mountains — Etc., Etc., Etc.

Chapter X...79
Hunting for Provisions — The Grizzly Bear — The Indian Devil — Deer and Antelope — Lose Another Wagon and Oxen — A Forest on Fire — "Pine Meadow" — "Pleasant Valley" — "Mount Shasta" — Short of Provisions — Kill a Buck — Meet with Indians — Lost in the Forest — Attacked by Indians — Hunting for the Trail — Etc., Etc., Etc.

Chapter XI 87
Meet with Indians — Bear River — The Indian and His Squaw — Arrival at "Fort Redding" — Tired and Hungry — The Cook and the Friendly Irishman — Leave the Fort — Arrival of the Train — Jim's Story — The Auction — Commence Mining — Bear and Bull Fight — Etc., Etc., Etc.

Chapter XII 96
Voting for President — Free Rum — In the Mines — The Rainy Season — Out of Flour — Dan and the Mule — Frightening the Indians — Parting with Old Companions — Meet with a Friend — In the Mud — Red Bluff — Arrive at Sacramento — Start for Weaver's Creek — Stockton — Out of Money and Provisions — Etc., Etc., Etc.

Chapter XIII 104
Indian Bread — Cold, Wet and Hungry — A Friend in Time of Need — In Search of Work — The Stanislaus River — Cross the Ferry — Still on the Tramp — In the River — The Government Surveyors — Arrive at the "American House" — Its Landlord — A Wild Look — A Kind Friend — "Uncle John's Eating House" — Etc., Etc., Etc.

Chapter XIV 112
The Gambling House — French Camp — Hungry and no Work — The Generous Captain — Start Again for the Mines — The Valley of the San Joaquin — Attacked by Robbers — "Food for Man and Beast" — Tuolumne County — Chinese Camp — Mining — Etc., Etc., Etc.

Chapter XV 121
My Experience in the Mines — The Panther — Build a Stockade — A New Arrival — Melons and Cucumbers — Baked Beans — A Surprise — The Good Book and its Effects — "Cleaning out the Tom" — Sell the Claim — Prospecting for a New Claim — Build a Log Cabin — The Stage Driver — A Sudden Departure — The Rainy Season — George and the Grizzly — Prospecting the Island — Etc., Etc., Etc.

Chapter XVI 129
Working out the Road Tax — Sonora — Hydraulic Mining — Surface Mining — "Spirit Hollow" — "I am Free! I am Free!" — Music and Gambling — Sunday in the Mines — Use of Quicksilver in Mining — Poison Oak — The Fox and the Rooster — An Unwelcome Visitor — The Alarm Signal — A Visit to Chinese Camp — Wood's Creek — Poverty Flat — Etc., Etc., Etc.

Chapter XVII 137
The Chinese — Sell Out and Leave the Mines — The Stage Driver Again — Stockton — Arrive at San Francisco — Start for Home — Virgin Bay — Virgin Lake — The San Joaquin River — The Rapids — The Steamer

Northern Light — Setting a Deadhead Ashore — Arrive in New York — Take a Bath — Scenes and Incidents in the City — Etc., Etc., Etc.

Chapter XVIII 144
Start for Boston — Meet Shaw on the Steamer — Arrive in Boston — "Must have Gold" — Leave for Chicago — The False Lover and his Punishment — Visit the Farm House — The Entertainment — The Departure — A Scene on the Train — Leave the Train — In Search Of Lodgings — Etc., Etc., Etc.

Chapter XIX 152
A Kindly Greeting — Illinois — The Population — Leave for the "Grand Prairie" — Arrive at Kankakee City — Meet "Sam" — The Disappointment — Return to Chicago — The Farmer's Exchange — The Letter — Start for Webster Creek — Sickness and Death of "Alice" — Arrive in New York — Home Again — The End.

The Cranberry Webb Worm 157

Appendix — John Fisk's Lineage 158

In Search of Gold

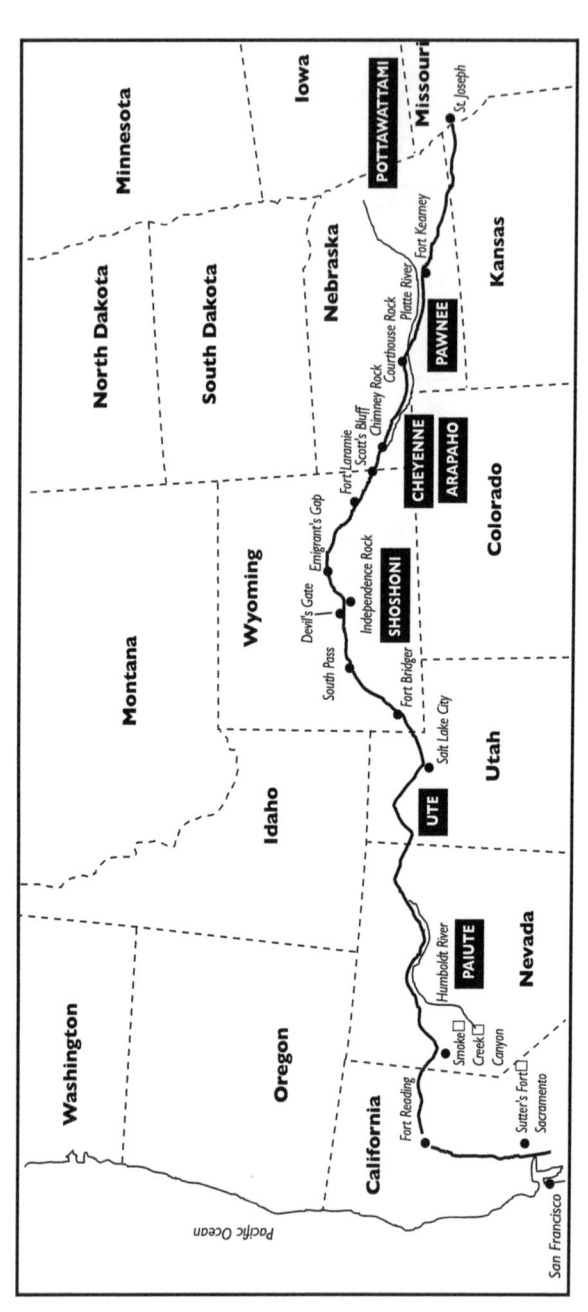

John Fisk's second journey to San Francisco was by wagon train and started near Kankakee, IL in April, 1852. Beyond St. Joseph, MO was largely Indian territory. The map shows nations and landmarks along the Overland Trail.

CHAPTER I

The Company — The Ship New Jersey and Her Outfit — The Start — Services on Board Ship — Killing Time with Ruta Bagas — Porpoises and Flying Fish — Dividing the Company into Messes — Shirking Duty — Duff and Soft Tack — The French Cook — "Man Overboard!" — Trade Winds — River La Plate — The Storm — Brazilian Fishermen — Staten Land — Preparations to "Round the Horn" — The Falklands and Tierra del Fuego — A Ruse, "Sail ho!" — In the Pacific — "Crossing the Line" — "Old Neptune" — A Terrible Storm — In Callao — A Visit to Lima, Peru — On Board Again — Arrival at the "Golden Gate" — In San Francisco — Start for the Mines — Etc., Etc., Etc.

In the years eighteen hundred and forty-eight and nine, when the papers were teeming with glowing accounts of the new El dorado where fabulous fortunes were being made in a day, and young and old were starting off without taking leave of their nearest friends, I took the gold fever, having arrived at that age (eighteen) when the love of enterprise is the strongest in the breast of man. Being on State Street, in the city of Boston, and seeing a large advertisement on the opposite side of the street that read "to sail in ten days for

3

California," was the very thing I was looking for. The agent said they were organizing a company of two hundred members, each member to pay two hundred dollars, making the capital forty thousand dollars; the company to be governed by a President, Vice-President, Secretary, Treasurer and eight Directors. They had bought the ship New Jersey, of six hundred and forty tons burden; her outfit consisted of the following articles: 300 barrels of flour, 300 barrels of beef, 200 barrels of hard bread, 300 barrels of pork, 600 pounds of coffee, 50 bags of salt, 25 barrels of sugar, three thousand dollars worth of medicines, 80 kegs of butter, 40 boxes of raisins, tools of all kinds, 20 horse-carts, 100 wheelbarrows; also lumber for a large house, all framed to put up at short notice; also three hundred thousand bricks, as ballast; and many other useful articles wanted in a new country.

We had quite a number of smart men in our company, some of them afterwards served in the legislature of the new State. There were four Morrills, five Merrills, three Crowells, two Sikes, and a Shad among the entire crew. To all appearances, it would seem that the company might live together in peace and harmony. There were 32 cabin passengers, mostly married folks; one gentleman from South Carolina, with two slaves, all the company had berths between decks; stowed pretty close together, and when in the warm latitudes it was quite uncomfortable you may know. On the first day of May, we hauled out into the stream and the next afternoon the sails were spread to the breeze, and when the sun had set in the ocean, land was no longer in sight. Some one hundred of us were quite busy throwing provisions overboard; no one said anything against it, however, it being considered a necessity when first going to sea. We stood up bravely, gold being our lode star, the main factor in most things with man. Some of us were seasick for nearly two months. The smell of bilge water and tobacco smoke made our lives anything but pleasant.

The second day we made a run of one hundred and seventy miles. In a few days more we were among the kelp, in the Gulf Stream; it rained most of the time while crossing it. On Sunday morning we held services on deck; a very good attendance considering the different nationalities on board. We had one hundred bushels of rutabaga turnips piled up on the forecastle; we ate a good many of them raw to fill up the time, and our stomachs too.

Monday it blew pretty hard. The question was asked by some one if we were almost there. Porpoises were playing in front of the bows; we saw a few flying fish and one came on board, said to be chased by the dolphins. We sail on day after day with nothing to gaze at but sky and ocean.

May 20th — Today Rio bears 120 miles to the West; did think of making the port, but it would occupy time, so kept on our course.

The company is divided into sixteen messes; each mess had a captain to keep them straight, and scrape between decks. The decks are scraped twice a week, and each mess take their turn; a good many would try to shirk and we would jerk them out with a rope, besides giving them a taste of the end. We also had a fire watch, two each night, with some soft tack to keep our eyes open. Thursday and Sunday were duff days. These were looked forward to with interest; the rest of the week the fare was salt beef and salt pork, and then salt pork and salt beef. We kept this up 168 days. The baker was a little Frenchman and his duff and soft tack were very good, but he was so very peculiar the ship's company were always making fun of him. One of the sailors tore off one of his coattails and he went to the Captain about it. He called all the sailors aft and made them toe a mark on the deck; then told the baker to point out the man. This was in the presence of all on board. The Frenchman pointed out and said, "That de man," all eyes were turned on him and the Captain told him what he could do with him, and would, if he heard any more such work.

Once in two weeks all hands were called up on deck, and their names were called over to see if any were missing. One day a man was out on the martingale trying to catch a "Spanish man-of-war," as they are called, a kind of jellyfish that floats on the surface. When passing the ship, they turn down on their side. The ship pitched more than usual, the man was washed off and the ship passed over him; it was soon known, however. "Man overboard" was heard throughout the ship, a boat was lowered, and the ship brought up to the wind, as soon as this could be done. By this time, the man was nearly a mile astern; he had got his boat off and was striking out for the nearest land three hundred miles distant.

We are now off the Brazils, running down the trade winds, which takes us along about seven knots an hour. This is the finest climate in the world; not a sail to be changed for twenty days, the wind blows from the same quarter every day. Saw two very large whales today; one of them threw himself almost out of the water, making foam like a cataract. It is said a swordfish is probing him underneath when he does this.

June 10th — We are now off the River Plate. About four o'clock in the afternoon this day, heavy black clouds rolled up from the Southeast and darkness began to set down rapidly; although the sun was quite high, the wind began to rise fast. Some of the light sails were sent down and everything was made as snug as possible. It soon blew a gale that whistled through the rigging; the lightning flashed incessantly, the roar of heaven's artillery was almost deafening, and the rain came down in torrents. About midnight we were forced to go below; the hatches were fastened down, and tremendous waves were coming on board. The storm broke about noon the next day; the sea was running very high. In the afternoon we saw a French ship on the weather beat with her fore and misen topgallant mast gone.

When off the Brazils we saw a catamaran, a raft of logs fastened together. There were two men on this thing fishing, about 11 miles from land; they had about a bushel of fish, which we bought for one dollar. They had been out about a month, they said.

June 23 — The "Magellan Clouds" had been in sight sometime; also the "Southeast Cross." At daylight, the joyful sound of "land ho!" was heard from the masthead; this proved to be the cheerless spot called Staten Land, covered with snow; it is now winter in this part of the world. At noon we were nearly abreast of it; it seemed so good for the eyes to rest upon after gazing so long at sky and water; at night it had gone. About nine o'clock there was a great commotion on deck; a large ship had just grazed the stern of our vessel, as good luck would have it, doing no damage, that would have been a

Chapter I

bad place to have been put down. Now the ship was made snug for the passage around the "Horn."

July 4th — The weather is very stormy and cold. We shall celebrate the day with cranberry tarts and a few speeches. I don't think there was an equal number of young men in the United States that used less rum and cold water. The rum was all gone and we were now on an allowance of a pint of water a day.

We have now been twenty-one days beating off the Falkland Islands and the cheerless land of Tierra del Fuego. Every morning each man comes up and gets his pint of water, taking his turn; this is a hard time for the water. The commissary must stand there two hours, with the mercury at zero, dealing out water, the ship pitching and rolling at a great rate, many a man not getting below with even a fill in his dish, the decks so slippery he is lucky to get down without a broken nose. One snowstorm and twenty-five snow squalls are the order of each day. We have no fire between the decks, so after breakfast we turn in; get up and get supper and turn in; get up and get dinner and turn in. We suffered greatly with chilblains for a month and a half. The captain tried many ways to get us on deck that we might get aired. One morning a man came to the companionway and sang out, "Sail ho!" We all rushed on deck but there was no sail to be seen; we were chilled dearly to the bone before we got down again.

We ran down to 59 1/2 South latitude; this point was reached at midnight. The next three days we had a tremendous snowstorm, directly aft. In four days we sailed one thousand miles. We are now well in the Pacific Ocean, and we can come on deck. The days are now five hours longer, and it is growing warmer every day.

August 15th — Juan Fernandez — the reputed home of Robinson Cruso — have in sight. This is quite a large island. In five days more we "crossed the line;" we lay becalmed five days, three degrees from the line; the pitch oozed from the deck, they were the hottest days I ever felt. "Old Neptune" came on board and made a great racket, and there came very near being a mutiny. Pistols were used, and it required all the force of the officers to quell the disturbance.

A large shoal of porpoises are now playing in front of the bows, and they are getting the harpoon rigged for the slaughter. The rope tied to the harpoon is run through a pulley block, then some forty men get hold, and when a porpoise is struck he is run up and pulled on board. Within an hour we had eight; they weighed about three hundred pounds; they tasted good after being kept on salt meat so long. The Cape pigeons and albatrosses follow in the wake of the vessel every day, unless it storms hard; the waves run mountains high all around the Cape. We spoke a large clipper ship bound to Calcutta; when we were in the trough of the sea she was mounted on a high wave. She looked immense, her bottom covered with shining copper.

August 18th — We had a terrible storm that lasted three days. About midnight a big wave struck the ship as we were laying to; we thought we were going down, and a good many of us were thrown out of our berths, and someone rang the bell; we were much frightened. The vessel had to be put before the wind; she was nearly on her beam-ends at one time.

August 28th — we made the port of Callao. The green land and the busy mart were a joyful sight to behold, and a run on shore we had been looking forward to for some time. There were quite a number of vessels in port at this time, some were bound for Calcutta and some for San Francisco. A great many years ago Callao was sunk by an earthquake; new Callao is a small place built higher up. The fort appears quite strong, although five hundred Californians took the place and held it for a day, for the fun of the thing. When we wanted to make an inspection, they would not let us come near. The fort is built in a half circle, with five terraces, each terrace mounted with twenty guns, having a good command of the harbor. One vessel tried to get out without paying harbor dues. She was nearly three miles off and they fired a gun with blank cartridge to bring her to, but taking no notice, they fired a shotted gun, carrying away her main topgallant mast that brought her to in a hurry. There was a large stock of wheat in bulk on the quay, which, to us, was a novel sight. It seems it never rains in the country; the land under cultivation is irrigated. We saw some crops just coming up, others half grown, and some ready for the harvest.

Chapter I

The third day in port ten of us went up to Lima, the capital of Peru. This is a walled city with four large iron gates, the same height as the wall, twenty feet; the streets are all paved with stones running at right angles, the sidewalks are paved with beams, the joint forming the surface, laid in all manner of devices, also in various colors; it is the neatest work I have ever seen.

No wheels are used in the streets; everything is packed on mules and asses, with jingling bells; the streets are quite silent. The place contains six hundred churches, said once to have been very rich. The mountain robbers have from time to time come down, broken down the gates, and carried off much of the church wealth. We went in to one church said to cover twelve acres of ground; it was 221 feet high with seven belfries, seven bells in each, making forty-nine bells, which could be heard a long distance.

We went to the market; it was in a wide street without any covering whatever; here was a row of fruit and vegetables, and another row of dry goods, silks, satins and cottons, all lying on the pavements without anything to protect them from the weather.

At four o'clock, we passed out at the eastern gate. In about a mile we came to the estate of one of the nobility; he was off on a foreign tour; his foreman let us come in and eat all the fruit we wanted for ten cents each; this was a great treat to us. Here we found oranges, lemons, limes and a great many other kinds of fruit that never leaves the country and is not known outside; also all kinds of nuts from the largest to the smallest, in every stage of growth. The ground was covered with all kinds of fruit, all going to waste.

At gunfire we went on board; this had been a great day of enjoyment. We had brought a large quantity of sand fleas on board in our clothes. These are horrid little imps that bit us until we declared again we would never set foot on shore again, and it was nearly two weeks before we saw the last of them. Here we saw the handsomest ladies in the world, and would have liked to kiss them, but good manners prevailed.

The fourth day we raised the anchor, and at sundown the land was not in sight. The second day we saw a sail dead ahead; at noon came up with her; she proved to be the Sea Eagle, from Boston,

In Search of Gold

bound to the land of gold, with one hundred persons on board, 160 days out; a regular old tub. We passed within two hundred feet of her, and went three rods to her one; both parties cheered incessantly while passing. In thirty minutes we were out of hearing, and at sundown they were hull down in the distance.

October 10th — The joyful sound of "Land, ho!" was heard, which proved to be the land of gold; at noon the "Golden Gate" came in view. As soon as the sea breeze set in, we made for the gate and passed through, up the bay five miles, and dropped anchor. Our voyage was up, one hundred sixty-eight days from Boston. In an hour a schooner from East Boston, loaded with lumber, dropped her anchor alongside of us; she sailed a day before us; we had not seen her on the passage. More than five thousand sails were in the bay at this time; almost every nationality of the world. There were not more than a dozen houses in San Francisco at this time, and these were drinking places of the lowest kind. In a few days, however, buildings began to go up rapidly, and in a month, quite a city was built.

The New Jersey was sold cheap, but her outfit brought big prices, but the officers proved everything but honest men, and we divided ten dollars each; it should have been four hundred dollars or more.

The third day after landing I went to work wheeling out gravel for a cellar at five dollars a day, five silver dollars paid into my hand each night. This seemed a big thing after working for ten dollars a month at home. I stayed here a week, then I took a man into partnership by the name of Read; he was out in the war of 1812. No one would take him, so I took him along. We bought a small outfit for the mines, and hired a passage up to Sacramento in a small schooner, where we arrived in due time. It had got to be near November, and the rainy season would soon commence. In two days the old gentleman was taken down with dysentery; this made it bad, and that night it commenced to rain; it seemed to come down in pailfuls.

On Saturday we hired a man to take our things up to Weaver's Creek, sixty miles distant, for ten dollars, the whole not to weigh over fifty pounds. I was sitting on a log Sunday morning, thinking

Chapter I

of my distant home, when a man came up to me and said, "Can you chop wood?" I said I could. "Well," said he, "I like your looks and will give you one hundred and fifty dollars a month, for two months." I said, "I am your man." He had hired another man and would not take my partner; he went with the things to the mines, and I did not see him again for a year. Our boss's name was Mark; his business was to deliver letters through the mines, receiving one dollar each. Monday morning Mark hired two sailors and their boat to take us down the river ten miles where we could find plenty of wood; the other man that was to work with me, whose name was Staggers, and well named he was, he had them quite often. It began to rain soon after starting, and rained all day. The two sailors were a rough set and were soon under the influence of liquor; the same with the other two. I then had to take the tiller and hold the sheet; it was a head wind and I was obliged to tack every little while. They tried to force some liquor down my throat and we had quite a tussle; nearly capsizing the boat. Just before dark they had become so crazy that they were dangerous, and so I run the boat full tilt into the brush and jumped on shore and left them to dance out their drunken reel. I saw a light a long distance off and went for it. I had not gone more than eighty rods when up jumped three grey wolves and glared at me, their eyes looking like fireballs in the darkness. I left but a few tracks in going back to the river. The men had got on shore and were trying to make a fire, and after a long time their efforts were rewarded with success; they then laid down on the wet ground and went to sleep. I made a bed on a couple of oars, to keep me out of the water in the boat. The rain came down in torrents until daylight, when it cleared up, and the men came on board, and we dropped down the river about a mile and went ashore, paced off one hundred and sixty acres of land, got some breakfast, dried our clothes, when we felt better. Mark and the two sailors started back in the afternoon. Staggers and I set up our tent and stowed our provisions that the wild animals might not get at them. The next day; we went to work to build us a cabin to keep the wild animals out, a tent being little or no protection against them. In two weeks we had the best cabin in the valley. We wanted about forty pounds of nails to build with. I started off one morning early for Sacramento, ten miles distant; at six miles I paid a Dutchman one dollar to take me across the river. In about a mile a man came up and I tried to keep up, but could not do it; he passed on like the wind and was soon out of sight. I never saw anyone walk so fast before.

Sacramento was a city of tents. I bought my nails for forty cents a pound and started back down the river, ten miles, with forty pounds of nails to carry through bear trails and deep sluices. After going six miles I heard a great commotion in the brush just ahead. After listening a short time, I threw my nails down and crept forward until I could see what it was. It was a panther; he had just killed a wild cow; he was so busy I was not seen and I crept swiftly back, picked up my nails and then took some pretty long steps for a mile or two, arriving at our tent about dark. Staggers was glad to see me; he said Indians had been around; he had seen them coming and hid in our cellar hole, covered with brush, until they had gone away. There not being much wood to cut, we commenced to grub up the bushes, with the intention of making it into a market garden, all kinds of vegetables selling very high at Sacramento. I had worked a month when Mark came down and brought two more men, Jones and Slambang, to work clearing up.

December 25th — These people keep Christmas with a vengeance! They had got a gallon of rot gut whiskey, and the way they drank it was a sin, and no mistake. Staggers staggered for a while, and then he couldn't; they fought, they drank, and quarreled for two days and nights; they all got hold of me and forced some of the fiery liquid down my throat; it burnt like fire. I went out and got an axe and got on a log and worked until I had sweat the stuff out.

CHAPTER II

The Sacramento River — Wild Animals — Wild Fowl — Start for Weaver's Creek — Hotel Comforts! — "Prospecting" — The Poisoned Spring — Sickness in Camp — The Funeral — A Queer Bedfellow — The "Mysterious Rider" — Return to the States — On the Isthmus — Etc., Etc., Etc.

February 15th — The river now began to overflow its banks, and in four days the valley was covered back for thirty miles. The cabin was built on a small rise of ground, a deep ditch on two sides. We built a dam in front, along the river, to keep from being washed away. Here we were confined in our cabin. For fifteen days Sacramento was no more; a great deal of property came floating down; we had no boat and it went past down to the ocean.

The steamer Senator made two trips a week from San Francisco to Sacramento; she made such big waves they tore down our dam every time she passed. As soon as we heard her coming we always run out with our shovels and commenced to dig. Small wolves, and large grey ones, lions and panthers and other animals passed in front of our cabin every night. There was but a narrow strip of land next the river that was not covered with water. One day I thought I would go up where we had last been at work to see if the water had gone down, that we might go to work again. Just as I turned around to return I heard something coming, it stopped. I thought it might be a deer; I had never seen one, and I whistled; it jumped over some high bushes fifteen feet I should think; it stopped again; I could not see it for the bushes; I whistled again, it gave two springs and came within six feet of me; it was no deer, I saw at once; it had a large head something like a bull dog, its body was dark brindle, with very stout limbs; its eyes blazed like coals of fire, he rolled his lips back showing some very white teeth, growling the while. I had nothing with me but an old jack knife, the blade of which would not stay in place, but I grasped it firmly, keeping my eye steadily fixed on the animal's blazing orb, and there we stood. Seeing he never flinched, I gave a tremendous scream and jumped towards him; he jumped back a little but did not run. I then made some pretty lively jumps back into deeper water and ran down the valley towards the cabin, the animal running parallel, about thirty feet off. I soon came to a ditch that made in from the river, about eight feet wide. I could not go up to the log near the river for the animal stood watching between, but I gave one of my biggest jumps, struck my toes on the opposite bank, wavered an instant, but luckily fell forward. I was now in sight of the cabin; two dogs were out hunting; they saw the lion and took to their heels, carrying their tails very low; the lion came no farther than the ditch. When I got down to the cabin, I told the men to take their guns and go for him, but they considered discretion the better part of valor. The valley being overflowed, the wild animals became dangerously hungry.

This is the country for ducks and wild geese — large flocks in sight all the time — the river is full of fish, too; we caught but a few, however, for we had only one small hook. Large herds of Spanish cattle roam the valley, the pasturage being excellent. Staggers shot a wild fowl one day and we salted it down; it proved very acceptable, our fare being flour, rice, and salt pork. Having worked two months and a half, and Mark not coming down on time, three of us quit work and went up to Sacramento. I had not received any money

Chapter II

since commencing work, and I felt quite anxious. We found the house where Mark put up, so concluded to stay there until Mark came down from the mines. The next day the city highway surveyor hired us to fell large sycamore trees to fill up the streets. Every night he paid us ten silver dollars; these made our overall pockets swing like a pendulum. It was not safe to leave anything at the boarding house.

In a few days Mark came and we received our pay; he offered me two hundred dollars a month for two months if I would stop, but I was bound for the mines; so we three on Monday morning early started for Weaver's Creek, sixty miles distant, packing our blankets and provisions. At night we camped under some live oaks; it rained and snowed all night. The best thing we could do was to lay and shiver until daylight. It continued to snow and rain all day and not being able to start a fire, our matches becoming wet, we went on twenty miles. I had taken a terrible cold that night, from which I suffered for some time. About four in the afternoon we came to King's Hotel, a single room, the ground for a floor, full of miners' tobacco smoke, lice and vile rum. We tried to dry ourselves before the fire and succeeded in a measure. After a while we got some supper, for which we paid one dollar and a half; he said if we could find a place on the ground not occupied, we might turn in there. The gamblers continued to play until midnight, drinking, fighting and swearing like fiends incarnate. Then we dug a hole in the tobacco juice, scraped away the pieces of flesh the gamblers had torn from each other, and turned in. We were soon peopled by millions of lice that bit and tore until daylight.

When we got up we got some breakfast, and then started down the creek to prospect for gold, the idol of man. We found a place we thought would pay; we bought a cradle and some tools, found a deserted cabin and took up our quarters there for a spell. It was raining almost every day, and the water being high, we only made five dollars a day apiece. We had to travel over quite a high mountain to get down to the place where we worked. Jones not being inclined to do his part of the work, we bought him out.

I and Slambang worked together about a month, making about

the same each day, living in the old cabin, sleeping on the floor, the earth.

I went out prospecting one day, and Slambang made some bread for the first time. When I got back, he had it set up all around the cabin. I told him he had better pave the ground with it, as it would not be possible to eat it. Pork cost us one dollar and fifty cents a pound. These we used very sparingly; our ten dollars a day would hardly furnish sufficient food for us — made slapjacks mostly, mixing in some Indian meal to make them light. At every meal I made a pile about eight inches high; placed on a shingle, cut down through the middle, then each man went to work until the last one had disappeared.

It now rained so hard every day we could work but little. Slambang came across a sailor, a former friend of his; he went up to King's rum shop quite often to see him, and did not return until the small hours in the morning, crazy with rum. One morning I told him I would sell or buy him out; he took the hint, and offered to sell his half of the tools for sixteen dollars. We shook hands and parted, I have not seen him since. He was a first rate man to work and a good companion when not in rum.

May 1st — I now went down to the river and tented with three other men, Samson, Donnelly, and Charles Stewart. Samson was a Southern fire-eater. Several of us built a dam to turn the water out of the main channel, that we might make a prospect, and it proved quite rich; got two dollars to the pan. After working several days three of us were taken down sick from drinking from a poisonous spring; the water was very clear and nice tasting, probably impregnated with some mineral. After we got out again, Donnelly said he should drink again, and did, against our advice. He was taken down the second time, and the third day he died. I was not well myself, neither Stewart, his brother-in-law, having had the chronic dysentery for one year, and not having done a day's work for that time. He wished to have me go and get the doctor some four miles down the Creek through the chaparral. It was nearly dark when I started and had not gone more than a mile when I heard something crashing through the brush after me. It followed me some two miles. I made

Chapter II

very quick time for that distance. Having arrived at the Doctor's tent I commenced to wake him up; this I found slow work, having been working hard mining all day; some of the others having awakened shook him up. He said he hardly wanted to go, there were so many bears around. He asked me if I had seen any coming down; I said only one. The boys urged him to go and do his duty, so we started back, arriving about midnight, the lions and panthers making the way scary with their horrid yells.

The next afternoon, towards night, Donnelly died. We laid him out as well as we could under the circumstances. We made a fireside of a log, I and the fire-eater keeping watch until daylight to keep away any wild animals that might be prowling around. Twice during the night we heard crashing in the brush quite near; we threw firebrands that way and heard them no more. The night wore away at last. I and Stewart being on the sick list, the fire-eater with three other miners, it being Sunday morning, started off to get some boards to make a coffin. They had to go four miles before they could find enough for the purpose; it was one of the hottest days of the season. At Sandy Bar, on the American River, it was 140 in the shade; several men died from the heat. It took seven men over an hour to dig the grave; each could work but a few moments at a time. When all was ready, we lowered him into his lonely grave.

One night when all four of us had been laying down about an hour, I felt something coiling itself up on my blanket over my knees. Said I, "Boys, there is a snake gone to sleep on my legs." They would not believe anything of the kind. I said, "Look out!" I then threw my feet up, the snake came down and struck the fire-eater in the breast. "Thunderation!" said he, and out we all ran. We lit a pine torch as soon as possible, but could find no snake. Fire-eater said he must have weighed four pounds; it nearly knocked the breath out of him. Not much sleep that night.

A man by the name of Snow opened a boarding house near King's. I thought I would board there a week at twenty-one dollars, with the privilege of sleeping on the floor; his grub was not much better than down at camp. When the dysentery once gets hold, it is hard to cure.

In Search of Gold

I had been making ten dollars a day; the water had got down and I was making at this time twenty dollars a day; this was the result from washing one hundred buckets of surface dirt. Three of us built a dam, which turned the water into a new channel. The first prospect we got two dollars to the pan. We thought with a good tom we could make one hundred dollars a day. I made ten dollars a day for a number of days, digging under a large sugar pine, where one must look twice to see the top. They have large cones the size of a two-quart measure, full of very nice nuts.

The snakes are very plenty all along the creek. I have seen more than a hundred at a time, copper heads; these with a ring around their necks; blowers, cotton mouths, racers, class snakes, bull snakes, rattlesnakes. One evening as I was washing out a pan of gold in a small pool of water, I happened to look across some three feet away; there lay a large rattlesnake just on the point of springing. I saw him none too soon. I stepped back and just cleared his bite. He then took after me; I went backwards and threw stones until my arm was lame. I hit him at last, as he was going over a stone, and nearly cut him in two. They are quite a lazy snake, but get over the ground faster than one would suppose.

During my stay here, Samson and I went prospecting up to Georgetown, Hangtown and so down on the American River but found nothing better than Weaver's Creek. On our return, we stopped at Georgetown. It was on Sunday night. A gambling house was to be opened that night, so we went to see the fun. They had not played thirty minutes before there was a terrible fight, and all the lights were blown out. We managed to get out without being shot.

Four miles from here there is a mountain on the American River that twelve men tunneled into some three hundred yards, struck the bed of an old river that proved very rich in pay dirt. They found gold that way. The first day they struck the bank of the river, they took out twelve thousand dollars, and it continued to pay the same for some time. These are considered big strikes. Many tunnels are dug that pay nothing and a great deal of labor is thrown away.

About this time, the "mysterious rider" was seen; also many mur-

Chapter II

ders were being committed, by whom, none could tell; the horseman was dressed in dark grey and was fully armed; whenever seen, it was always at evening or just before day. A company of miners were organized on the fifteenth of May to put a stop to so many murders. No one felt, when he laid down at night, that he would ever rise again. We started off in all directions, and for four days hunted high and low, but with no success. The next night two miners in our own camp were murdered, and two thousand dollars in gold dust taken. After this a string was tied at the front of each tent at night, with a stone and a tin pan tied together, so that if anyone came in the tent the pan would ring and give the alarm. The third night two shots were heard at one of the outside tents and a Mexican "Greaser" was killed.

Charles Stewart and I having been sick for a long time with the dysentery, and getting worse every day, the doctors charging seventy dollars a visit, we concluded to return to the States. Not being able to sell any of our things, we were obliged to leave them where they stood; so one bright morning in June we went up to the hotel and engaged our passage to Sacramento, sixty miles distant. The next morning, when it was the color of a grey cat, we started to ride sixty miles, on the bottom of a wagon that rested on the bare axles. In our condition, it was something we shall never forget. We arrived about five in the afternoon at Sacramento, got a little supper, and then went on board the steamer "Lapwing," that started out at six for San Francisco, one hundred and fifty miles distant, where we arrived at four o'clock the next morning. This place had been burned twice in my absence, with my chest and outfit for two years, the two pounds of powder giving my things quite a rise in the world. Every time the city is burned it is built better next time. It is now quite a large place, Montgomery street being the main thoroughfare. I paid a weeks board at the American House. The man said if the vessel sailed before the week was out he would return the balance. We had cots to sleep on instead of the floor. We were soon covered with fleas, and a few bedbugs thrown in, that we might not sleep too sound. We hired a passage to Panama, in the bark Drummond, at one hundred and fifty dollars each, Captain Sands, fourteen passen-

In Search of Gold

gers, and ballasted with coconuts. We had quite a pleasant passage, played euchre most of the time, living on sea air and hot biscuit, with a sprinkling of "old horse," as the sailors call it.

We arrived at Panama the twentieth of July, making the passage in one month and three days. On the strand lay a seventy-five foot whale that a storm a week before had left high and dry. About fifty natives, with quills, were sucking the fat from the carcass. Such an intolerable stench filled the air that the buzzards flew away in disgust. About four o'clock in the afternoon there came up a squall blowing very hard. Two vessels were at the offing; one came in just clearing the promontory, but losing almost every sail; the other went down with all on board.

I am quite sick with the dysentery, and how to get across the Isthmus, I don't know in my weak condition; but I must try and go with the rest. The next morning early we started out, some on horses and others on mules and asses; it was my bad fortune to have one of the latter. I was obliged to pay sixteen dollars for the privilege or go on foot. For the first few miles there were quite a number of nice gardens and cultivated lots; sometimes we would plunge into deep sloughs that were almost impossible for the animals to get through; the rest of the boys galloped on to the Half Way House and left me to get on the best I could, it put me in such pain to trot that I was obliged to let the animal walk. Once I came to a place that was five feet perpendicular, and not seeing the place where they turned off to go around, I concluded to go ahead, provided I could get the Jack down. I got off and coaxed the animal as near the edge as I could, and then gave him a sudden jerk, and he came down like a cat, right side up; I then mounted and went on. When I reached the Half Way House, the boys were just coming out, having had their dinner. I told them they must wait for me, which they did, I being the third from the hindmost man, travelling in single file, the man on the white horse taking the lead. We paid a native one dollar to guide us through.

CHAPTER III

Down the Chagres River — Stop at Havana — Cholera on Board Ship — Arrival at New York — "Home Again" — A New Start — Going West — Among Sharpers — On the Canal — Rochester — Cleveland — Chicago — Farming on the Prairie — Corn Planting — Building a House — Wild Pigeons — Etc., Etc., Etc.

At about dark we entered the cut in the ledge from three to eight feet deep; the night was very dark, the man on the white horse was perfectly invisible, and so we travelled on. The roar of the lions and other animals made our animals tremble with fear; the hissing of large serpents seemed close by us. About midnight we arrived at Crucees, on the Chagres River; here was a shanty called a hotel, kept by an American black man; he gave the boys some baked beans and charged them one dollar each; I managed to get a slice of toasted bread. We then lay down on the floor where the Spanish fleas done their terrible work. We soon ascertained that one of the boys had not come up, so the next morning the brother of the missing man went back part way to see what had become of him, but could not see or hear any sign of him, and he never came up; he being the hindmost man probably was devoured by some wild beast.

Four of us hired a dugout and two natives to paddle us down the river to Chagres, a seaport on the Atlantic side, the distance being seventy miles. One of the boys was perfectly helpless with rheumatism and lay flat on the bottom of the dugout; when we had made ten miles, one of the darkies refused to work and we set him on shore. The water of the river is as yellow as saffron, quite often an alligator would jump or slide into the river; the current is about four miles an hour. About dark there came up a terrible thunder shower; the water came down in pailfuls, the lightning was continuous, the thunder was terrific; it seemed as though the world could not hold together one hour more if it had kept on. By constant bailing we managed to keep afloat.

About eleven o'clock at night we arrived at the dirty little place called a port, wet as drowned rats. I managed to get a piece of toasted bread; it was all that I needed in my present condition; I paid a dollar for my supper and the floor for a bed. An old she goat kept running up and down the roof all night, also the fleas, bed-bugs and lice marched and counter-marched up and down the ossified railway of my back. The next morning we were rowed out to the steamer Georgia nearly rotten. This is not much of a harbor; the waves running high, one boat was swamped, losing two men.

In the afternoon we up anchor and start for the States. We made a stop of eight hours at Havana; before entering the port with two officers to demand our passports. The Captain said he had no passport; he was only waiting for a permit to enter the inner harbor to take in coal to last them to New York. After waiting some three hours the permit was sent on board. We then steamed in; it was nearly night when the coal barge came alongside, the native blacks were employed to get it on board. As each basket of coal comes on board it is emptied below with a yell from the blacks; this was kept up all night. At seven the next morning we had four hundred tons on board. Four great black policemen stood on guard to keep out the wharf thieves; two got on board, however and were caught by the passengers and a thumb taken from the right hand of each and then let go; glad were they to get off so well.

Chapter III

The third day from Cuba one of the cabin passengers was taken sick with the cholera. He was brought down in the steerage and laid on the floor. I never saw a man suffer so much as he did; the ship's doctor covered him with bags of hot salt, but all to no purpose. In two hours from the time he was taken he was a dead man; he was sewed up in a piece of canvass, with fifty pounds of iron fastened to his heels, then the corpse was placed on a door used for such occasions, and carried to the gangway. The vessel was then stopped; the chaplain then stepped forward and read the funeral service. At the word we committed the body to the deep; the corpse slid from the door and then down in to the mighty deep. It seemed to me very solemn, taking place as it did at the hour of midnight. In five minutes the vessel was under way as though nothing had happened.

We had a very pleasant passage to New York, where we arrived on the morning of March twenty-eight. Here I and Charles Stewart shook hands and parted, he going to New Jersey where his family lived. At five o'clock in the afternoon we went on board the steamer Sundown, for Fall River, where we arrived at midnight. Not feeling well, I took one of the lower berths. I had not been asleep more than an hour when I felt a hand in my pocket; I grabbed the hand of the thief and held on until he had dragged me out on the deck; he then got away; as I had lost nothing I let the scamp go.

We now took the cars for Boston, where we arrived at nine the next morning. I stopped here a few days and then went to Medford, from whence I had started eighteen months before. I stopped there over winter and in April I and another young man, a smith by trade, concluded to seek our fortunes in the far West; so we fitted ourselves out with a chest of tools and one good rifle, clothing for two years, and such other things as might come handy in a new country. We went by rail from Boston to Albany. We left the cars on the east side of the river and crossed the bridge on foot; when near the middle we met about forty runners; one of them grabbed Sam's carpet-bag and told him he could take him where he could buy a ticket for Buffalo cheaper than anywhere else. Sam thought it was all right and I could not prevail on him to think otherwise; one tried to get my valise and I tripped him up and hurried after Sam; the fellow ran up

In Search of Gold

Maiden Lane, to No. 6, and up into an office; here again I told Sam it was nothing but a bogus affair and we should lose our money. The man in the office stated we could go quicker, and he would give us a ticket two dollars less. Sam said he should buy a ticket, and not wishing to separate, I bought one also. After paying twelve dollars we got our tickets and read them over; instead of going by rail, for which we had paid our money, we had received tickets to go on a canal boat four hundred miles up the Erie canal to Buffalo; this was a damper; we had not filled the ticket in full, so we went to the Mayor for redress. He said he could do but little for us; we had paid our money, however, he said he would go down and make him fill the ticket out, which he did. I have never had the least doubt but the man received his part of the profits. I had it from good authority that the foreign element are badly swindled in this way. Sam said he would sell himself for about two cents; it was an entire new chapter in Sam's experience.

The next day we took our effects down to the canal boat and handed our tickets to the captain. "Why," said he, "there is nothing said about your board, and three meals a day for ten days is quite an item." We began to think so too; "However," said he, "I will do the best I can. I will board you for the trip for two dollars each;" this we willingly paid. The captain and his wife were very nice people and we enjoyed the trip very much. There are a good many large places all along the canal that are wide awake for money making. There is no Sunday here; storehouses and drinking saloons take in all sorts of goods. I and Sam frequently got off and walked; we could get on faster than the horses on the two-path, then when we got tired we would sit down and wait for the boat to come up. This canal is a big thing with its high embankment and numerous locks; one place called Lockport having eight locks; the boat going into one, the gate is shut and the water is let in from the one above; this raises the boat up fourteen feet, and so on until we arrive on the canal above, more than one hundred feet. Boats are passing up one side, others going down on the other side most of the time. Night and day boats are in sight most of the time throughout the entire length of the canal, and in many places crowded; twice we were wedged in tight and it required boats' hard work, six fights and any amount of hard words before we got started.

Rochester is in sight and is quite a large place. This is the place for rapping to call out spirits of the past, also spirits present, much worse than any of the other world. As any one can see along the line of this canal, it is a grand sight to see the flights of pigeons; from seven o'clock until about ten the sky is darkened with them; and then late in the afternoon on their return to their roosts. Large numbers of ducks and geese were continually passing over. The land all along the canal seems quite fertile. At the station saw mill a fine span of matched horses became frightened and jumped into the mill pond; having martingales on they could not get their head up out of the water and were drowned not more than fifteen feet from shore. Eighteen thousand horses are required on the tow path every day; they make a change of horses every twelve miles; two and three horses are used to draw each boat of from five to fifteen tons burden. In going around a bend the captain slewed the boat too near the shore; it canted on a stone tearing a hole in the bottom. The water coming in quite fast we manned the pump, Sam and I, and worked nearly all night, until we came up the repair ways, where the boat was left high and dry. We found a hole nearly four inches long. The next two days took us to Buffalo; this is a place that one must get out of the way or be run over; it is quite a stirring place.

We now went on board the steamer Lady-of-the-Lake, and presented our tickets to Chicago. The captain said we paid for a steerage passage only; he said we must pay two dollars more to go in the cabin. We concluded to go between decks and investigate. The first thing I observed of much interest was two old bruisers fighting, one had the other's [text obliterated], and he was trembling with agony, still he held on. The next thing that attracted my attention was four large body lice walking unconcernedly over the collar of a Dutch girl. The place was filled with tobacco smoke and the aroma from unwashed clothing. I said, "Sam, how is this?" He said, "You can go ahead after this." "Well," I said, "we had better pay the four dollars more and take cabin passage." The captain laughed and said we were not the first ones that had been sold in that way.

In Search of Gold

The second day we stopped at Sand Hill to wood up; it is on the Canada side, and the captain said we could have an hour to run on shore. A short distance inland several acres of oak ship timber had been cut down and hewed where it fell; all of them were very large, some were three feet square and 100 feet long. We ran over these like so many squirrels. It is splendid sailing over these Lakes, often in sight of cities and towns.

We stopped at Cleveland to leave a few passengers and freight; we were here nearly three hours. A number of us went out to the market, some two miles out of town, along side of a rail fence; this was decidedly new to us; of all the looking men and women, wagons and fixtures, in fact it beat the Dutch and something more. The country through here is quite rolling and seems well cultivated. A man by the name of Sampson, not a very strong man, however, on our return to the steamer went out into the fields some little ways and fell into a pit fall, seven feet deep, made to take Coyotes. Sam saw him go down and called to us that a man had gone out of sight very sudden. We all ran as fast as the nature of the ground would admit. Three of us came to the hole; we found Sampson trying his lungs at their best and we soon got him out. As we started for the road we heard another of the boys calling to us to help him out; we helped him out and he was so frightened that he could hardly stand; all this took up time. We now had to hurry back to the steamer; when within half a mile we heard the steamer's whistle and the bell ring; we all of us made fresh spirt, opened our safety valves, and went over that half mile about as quick as most folks. When we arrived at the pier the steamer, with our tickets and baggage, was nearly a mile out on the lake, Milwaukee being the next stopping place. The next morning about 7 o'clock the steamer Fire-Fly came in; we engaged a passage to Chicago, where we arrived in due time.

Chicago is quite a place and growing fast; nearly fifty buildings going up at the present time. The buildings are low and mostly of wood, a fire would be apt to sweep them clean; they are obliged to plank their streets to keep out of the mud; this will make it bad for a fire if one takes place. In a few days we got our luggage, shook hands with our late companions and started for the grand prairie,

Chapter III

sixty miles distant; here we soon found an odd section of land that suited us very well. The government gave the Illinois Central Railroad Company every other section of land, four miles each side of the line, to build the road. We expected in time this land would become valuable.

The roads over the prairie, winter and spring, are very bad, mud everywhere. It had now got to be the first of May. They commenced to turn over the prairie sod the 10th of May; quite a growth of grass has sprung up and this is turned under and the sod soon decays. Sam and I built a shanty to live in until we could put up a house. The next Saturday afternoon we went out to a Dutch farmer and bought a yoke of oxen for sixty-five dollars, six-foot cattle. The next day we bought a pair of stags for forty dollars; with this team we could turn over a sixteen inch sod three inches deep; it decays faster to turn it over shallow. We started from the shanty and ploughed forty rods long; in twenty days we had turned over twenty acres, some few "hard heads" in the way; this is a term used here for rocks. It is necessary to carry a file to keep the point of the plough sharp, as the sod is quite thick. As we kept going round the snakes became quite thick; when the last land was twelve feet wide we made a stop to kill the rattlesnakes; we killed fifteen that had gathered in on the twenty acres besides lots of others; among them was the glass snake, having the appearance of glass very much; wherever we strike one it breaks off short like glass; it is said they will return and attach themselves to the piece broken off.

The first of June we began to plant the corn in this way: with an axe we would strike into the sod every three feet and every third furrow, dropping the corn in the aperture made by the axe, stepping on it and closing it up; in this way we were three days in planting twenty acres. The corn came up and grew without any further attention, producing about forty bushels of shelled corn to the acre. When we had got our corn all planted, we dug the cellar for the house. There were no stones to build a cellar wall, so we put down a post at each corner some two feet below the cellar bottom, and on these we fastened the sills; those we obtained leave to cut on the "School Section," as we were to become settlers.

In Search of Gold

June 10th — We started with two teams for Wilmington, at the head of the Peoria Canal, and on the Kankakee River. Here we bought boards, laths, shingles, brick and lime. The third day we arrived at the shanty. We were in a hurry to get our house up on account of the mosquitoes; to say they were thick would not express anything of their numbers. At night fall the shanty would be crowded without any standing room for Sam and I, so every night before we turned in we made a smudge of dry cow chips; this drove them out and we went in and shut the door; then we had to cover ourselves up and nearly roast with heat in order to have any blood left in the morning. The next day a thundershower came up and blew so hard it took a board from the roof of the shanty and carried it up in the air; when it came down it was kindling wood. We built our house of boards planed on one side and matched; this is what they call a balloon house. The winds blow very hard out on the prairie, with nothing to break it off, and will often blow a house over; one built like this can be tipped back again; I and Sam worked on the house most every day. Through June and July we cut fifteen tons of hay; good grass over the whole country, no lack of hay. We put it into three stacks. We had one cow; I made between seven and eight pounds of butter per week. I churned it in an earthen jar; usually it would come in fifteen minutes, yellow as gold, and free from any bad odor. I also made a few cheese, but they were rather tough. The natural grasses will yield one and a half tons to the acre, and it makes very good hay. I had a shotgun and Sam had a rifle; we could get a prairie chicken any time, or ground plover; both are nice eating. I sowed half an acre of buckwheat; the third of July the pigeons came on it so thick I had to stand out there to keep them off. The next day being the glorious Fourth, I opened fire on the pigeons on the ground, on the rail fence, in the air, and finally set up a long pole and took them lengthwise. I soon had all my pots, jars and tubs salted down, filled to overflowing, but I soon found they were not good that way.

The water around here is bad; the soil lays on a strata of limestone. This makes the water hard.

July 20 — We wanted some place to keep our animals, so early

Chapter III

Wednesday morning we started for the barrens and cut some timber and poles, taking home a good load, where we arrived about night fall, tired and hungry. We had two prairie chickens in the pot with some fried potatoes and bread; after eating heartily we turned in. The next morning when we opened our eyes two tramps stood looking in from the doorway. I jumped up and said, "What do you want?" "Something to eat," they both said. I said, "We don't keep a tavern, nevertheless you shall have something to eat; but first go and take off that load of timber from the wagon." They went out and I have not seen them since. In about a week we had up quite a barn for this part of the country. Here we kept our oxen, cows and hens. The hens laid every day. Quite often I would see a grey owl up in the loft watching for mice. The coyotes would come around quite often and give off their dismal howl; often we were obliged to go out and give them a shot that we might get some sleep.

CHAPTER IV

Stray Cattle — Fear and Ague — Prairie Fires — The Corn Harvest — A Blizzard — Start Again for California — Crossing Prairie — A Rich Grain Country — Camping Out — Fellow Travellers — Starved Rock — Loss of One of the Party — A Terrible Hail Storm — Crossing a River — The Patent Grist Mill — Blacks at Work — The Amazon and her Turkeys — The Panther — Attacked by a Cougar — Etc., Etc., Etc.

August 12th—Our cattle strayed away and were gone three days before I found them; they were some ten miles away. When I returned home to the shanty the third day I was quite sick with a good deal of fever. Said I, "Sam, I am going to have the fever and ague from the way I feel." Sam was getting supper. Said I, "Sam, I don't want anything to eat, but make me a quart of composition, and have it hot." I got into bed under four quilts and five blankets; I then got down all the composition I possibly could, and the way that fever and ague walked out of my bones was a caution. I stayed under those blankets just ninety minutes; it has never dared to trouble me since. Sam was taken with it, and it did not leave him for

Chapter IV

years. One day he would have the fever, the next the chills; he could neither eat, sleep nor work; he said he would rather be dead than to live in such misery. I felt thankful I got out of it so slick. I think the cause is bad water and a miasma arising from so much new land being turned up. Our house is all finished but painting; we have moved in and now feel quite safe from our enemies, the mosquitoes. We felt bad to leave the shanty, and could not but feel a little homesick; this soon wore away as we became used to our new quarters.

September has come, and also these terrible prairie fires that I have heard of but had never seen until now. For a few days past we had heard rumors that the prairie, 50 miles to the westward, was on fire; it is said the hunters set the fires. The next day we ploughed around five acres some twelve feet wide, to keep it from being burnt. We intended to save this to burn the next June for the cattle to go on to when not feeding. The green head fly is a great bloodsucker, and their name is legion, but will not go on to a piece of land that has been recently burnt over. That evening we could see a wall of fire for a long ways; the second day at two in the afternoon it came down upon us like an evil spirit, bringing a strong breeze as it swept through the sloughs where the grass stands six feet high; the roar of the flames was tremendous, it was one grand cloud of flame and smoke before which ran for their lives cattle, horses, grey wolves, coyotes, deer, antelopes, snakes, and prairie hens, leaving the land covered with the drapery of mourning. The flames swept up to the rail fence and into the corn field some twenty feet, but did no great damage; it came very near getting into the house and hay stack enclosure, by a narrow strip not more than three by six feet. I was obliged to lay down and roll the fire out. I received a little scorching, losing a few whiskers; my clothes took fire but Sam was on hand to put it out. The fire went snapping by, down through the barrens, until it reached the river some six miles to the east of us.

October, and now the corn harvest begins. Sam and I take two rows each, with a sharp wooden pin fastened to the palm of the hand; with this the husk is readily separated and the corn gathered quite fast. We husk all day, throwing the corn in heaps on the ground; in the afternoon we gather it up, throwing it into a large bin built of rails; when full it is covered over with a stack of hay; here it dries and keeps well. We were about thirty days gathering sixteen hundred bushels of ears. It became very monotonous long before we had it all in. November, and the cold comes on the tapir; we want to fence eighty acres next year, so we go every day to the barrens to cut posts and rails. The third day Sam's hands were well blistered; he seemed to think there was a good deal of work in chopping, so he concluded to go down to Chicago and work at his trade. This left me to keep bachelor's hall all alone, except a yellow dog we had taken in as a stray. The winter, most of the time, was quite pleasant. I had some three weeks that I improved drawing logs on a sled from the barrens to be split into rails; by the first of March I had nearly two hundred dollars worth of fencing. When Sam came back he had earned eighteen dollars.

January 8th — We had a very cold blizzard lasting 4 days; no such thing as going out while it lasted, except to feed the cattle; the cold penetrated into the cellar, freezing every potato, some thirty bushels, I think. The mercury went down to five below zero. I have never felt the days to be so long before or since; no neighbors within three miles, and some of these I wished had been much further away.

Our combined capital by this time had dwindled down to a small sum. The best outlook for making money at this time was by stock raising, that requiring considerable capital. I said, "Sam, I will go across the Plains to California and get some money, while you stay here and look after things." This he agreed to do. There was a company forming at Reno, on the Kankakee River; with them I bargained for a passage across the Plains for 150 dollars; I sold them one yoke of oxen and wagon. The company consisted of seven able-bodied men, Bailey, Foster, Reed, Bruce, Vernotten, Salter, and Fisk as passenger. On the morning of April 15th, 1852, I shook hands with Sam and the few neighbors that had gathered to see us off on our perilous journey with our six yoke of oxen, two wagons, two heifers for milk, four shotguns, two rifles, a good supply of ammunition, picks, shovels, crowbars, besides a supply of cooking utensils. We laid in a supply of provisions, such as flour, bacon, coffee, enough to last to the confines of civilization, St. Joseph, some six hundred miles distant. We travelled today fourteen miles, and camped just outside of the little town of Wilmington. The next thing was to get some supper, which none offered to; they all said they had never cooked any. This was a dilemma; having paid my passage I did not care to work it, but seeing we should get no supper I said I would make the bread, Jim said he would make the coffee and try the bacon; this continued to the end of our journey.

We are now travelling across the grand prairie; here it is very level, the ducks and wild geese are very plenty, also ground plover. I shot two prairie hens and plover enough for us all a good supper. Today we travelled eighteen miles and camped along side of a woodpile; the farmer told us we might camp there if we would not steal anything. I told him we were not petty thieves, but wholesalable robbers, and if we saw anything of him out of doors again that we would give him a dose of pistol powders. In about an hour we sat down on the ground around the pot containing our chicken soup, each one helping himself, the one that got the most was the best fellow; the way the bones cracked was a caution to those that have no teeth. The next morning we got up, got breakfast, yoked our cattle and started on four miles; we came to the River Merson, a small stream that helps drain the grand prairie; this day we travelled twenty-three miles. All this section of country is level, and this time of year very wet; fever and ague is the ruling disease and hangs on in many cases to the bitter end. Tonight we camped on the side of the road near a farmhouse, where we bought hay and corn for our cattle, paying fifty cents a bushel for corn, twenty-five cents a hundred for hay. The small pox is raging fearfully, though her cleanliness is not the western forte by a long shot.

This is a great country for grain of all kinds; when the land is first broken up it is planted to corn two years, then oats one year, it being too rich for wheat. In some places I see the farmers are making some attempt at drainage; this will be a great improvement on the Rosin-weed lands; they are much richer than the higher grounds. There are no roads and we must tramp through the mud, raining most every day; this makes it very disagreeable travelling.

In Search of Gold

The next day we travelled sixteen miles; we camped in the woods. This is Saturday; we are now within five miles of Otterway [Ottawa]; here we shall wait for another train of six wagons. The man that lives here is a gentleman, that is also his name, and he is a gentleman in each sense of the word. He has one of the finest farms I have seen in this part of the country; it is high rolling prairie. There are about ten acres of orcharding just coming into bearing, one hundred acres of woodland, mostly ash and walnut; this is very valuable and we seldom see anything of this kind on the grand prairie, six hundred acres under cultivation; he holds it at ten thousand dollars. Here is a chance to make money even at that price.

Here comes a black covered wagon, three men and five yoke of oxen; we shall have them for fellow-travellers; two of the men are brothers, Richard and Edward Fuller, two of the most comical men that I have ever had the good fortune to have for companions. The boys soon found their weak points, and you may believe they made a good amount of sport. The one great thing that troubled Richard was we told him that his wife would marry another man while he was gone; we told him a number of such cases have happened, and we thought he might be visited with the same misfortune, and he took all in earnest. It was very entertaining to hear him tell what a pretty wife he had; he would hold up his hand three feet from the ground and say she was so tall, with black hair and blue eyes, and then would burst out and look so woe begone, saying what fool he was ever to start on so perilous a journey, that made us boys laugh long and loud. The third man went by the name of Parker, a six-footer, dark complexion, with a most disagreeable and savage look, but after a short acquaintance we liked him the best of the three. In two days' travel we came to the Mississippi Valley, travelled up six miles where we found plenty of grass for the first time since we started.

Early Monday morning we start on our journey, five miles. We came to the Illinois river; they charged us one dollar for ferry. Otterway lies on the opposite bank; it is a very pretty place. A good deal of business is done here, several small factories are in full blast. Here we met a large train of Californians with twenty-three wagons, but we hurried on that we might leave them far behind; here we laid in a supply of hotdrops and other medicines for the journey, in three miles we came to Sulphur Springs; very strong now. We are nearly opposite Starved Rock, where during the Indian wars, three thousand were kept on this rock by another tribe until they all died from starvation. The rock forms an elbow in the river, three sides of it are perpendicular, the river washing its base; here we saw a train of Mormons encamped, some two hundred or more; they were going to Salt Lake; they intend to take two seasons for the journey. It now began to rain, and we had some four miles to go before we could find a place where we could get corn and hay. We sent out a forage party, and in about an hour they brought in a supply, with two dozen eggs; with these, and two prairie hens, we made a very good supper. One of our boys was taken ill; it was a cold wet night and we had him carried to a farmhouse that stood out in the fields. One of the boys sat up with him all night and towards morning he sent for us all to come. He said, "Boys, my journey is ended. I am about to cross the dark valley where the wicked cease from troubling and the weary are at rest, and when you arrive at the land of God if there is anything left to my share send it home to my family." This they promised to do; he then bid all farewell and we left him there.

The next day we passed through Peru and Lassell [La Salle], two small towns within half a mile of each other; through the streets of the villages the mud is two feet deep. From here we travelled four miles, when there came up a terrible hailstorm that obliged us to take shelter in a farmyard from the violence of the storm. In a few moments two other trains came rushing in. It stormed all night and we all passed a most miserable night. The next morning early, our three teams rolled out and at sunrise we were four miles on our way. Today we passed many fine farms of large extent. This is a beautiful country. The land is rolling and dotted with quite large patches of timber; the land is more valuable where there is timber, so much is required for fencing it becomes quite an item in the farm account.

The next two days we travelled in mud. We have now before us two hundred miles of level, wet and unhealthy country, stuffed full of fever and ague, small pox and cholera. The people here are obliged to build their cabins of logs, on account of their shaking disease, the ague.

The next day, the first of May, we crossed the river in a ferryboat at Burlington; two other trains crossed at the same time. Burlington is quite a large place, built mostly of brick; it stands on a steep hillside; there is one good thing about it, the streets are very dry. Today is Sunday, and we shall observe the day by camping over until Monday morning, wash and mend our clothes. We had a large Newfoundland dog that belonged to Dan Vernotten; he proved a good friend on many occasions during our march across the plains.

On the tenth of May, we crossed the Des Moines River, at Farmington, quite a large place and quite a number of new buildings going up. They were at work on their first bridge over the river, the only one we saw in passing through the three States. Up on the hill above the town is the cemetery; here we viewed the graves of the pioneers of the State, and here there seemed to be a competition between two of the old school while in the flesh, and the same spirit followed them to the grave. On one of the headstones it read, "Here lies John Rug as snug as a bug in a rug." On the other, "Here lies John Rugger, darn sight snugger than that other Bugger." On one stone was cut the age, one hundred and eleven, quite a number had seen a hundred years.

We crossed the river on the ferry. On the other side our route lay through a forest, and here we went out of our way six miles, which was very unpleasant. In going that distance we crossed a small stream about waist deep, six times, and some of the boys would get behind and have to wade every time. Once when we were on the point of crossing it for the fifth time, Jim came running with all his might and gave a jump to reach the wagon; the driver whipped up the team and Jim fell into the water all over, to the great delight of the company. Jim was hopping mad; pistols and guns were brought out but no great damage done.

The turn of the road brought us in sight of what we took to be the part of a mill without any covering. The hopper and stones, and a man turning in a bag of corn. One of the boys asked the tiller whose invention that was. "Oh," said he, "that is a natural production."

Chapter IV

The people here seem rude and lawless, regardless of others' rights, as we found to our cost by the loss of one of our heifers that gave milk; this was a serious loss, affecting our bill of fare all the way through.

From here we travelled three miles, crossed over a brook, and we were in Missouri. Here we camped for the night alongside of a farmhouse, where we bought some eggs for five cents a dozen. The boys made what they called "egg-nog;" it was not bad to take; the only trouble is we seem to want more. Here we began to inquire the distance to St. Joseph. They told us it was two hundred miles and we began to despair of ever getting there, for we had no idea it was so far. This day we passed through two very pretty villages, the first we had seen in Missouri. We stopped in Augusta about an hour; four or five of us were standing in front of the tavern talking. I had noticed a black girl dodging her head out at the door on the opposite side of the street; she looked at Jim mighty cross, thinking he was making fun of her, and she said, "If you are talking about me you are talking about those that are far your superiors," and saying this went back into the house.

Today we saw a large number of blacks at work in the fields as we passed along and they all seemed to enjoy themselves very much in their own peculiar way. Their agricultural tools were very rude and weighty implements, and must require a large amount of muscular force to use them. We inquired of one planter why they were made so heavy; he said the slaves would break them if they could, that they might get rid of work.

The next day we travelled across a prairie thirty miles, without a house or a bush and here we encamped for the night near a cabin. We inquired the distance to St. Joseph and they said they did not know, but kinder [sic] reckoned it was two hundred miles and we found out the next day it was only thirty. The people here seem not very well informed and they seldom go beyond their own smoke; they wonder how folks can live so far from the center of the world.

The next morning we rolled out and the first cabin we came to there was quite an excitement; it seemed that a train of Californians had just passed; the old man was not at home at the time and some of the boys wanted to buy a turkey; the old lady refused to sell one, but the boys were bound to have one at any cost, and so they shot one and then ran out into the road, the old lady after them with the gun. When she came to the road she up and fired and shot one of the men, giving him an ugly wound that disabled him from going to California this season. When we came by she came out saying she had another gun loaded if we wanted to kill any more of her poultry. We told this Amazon we considered discretion the better part of valor, but one of the boys bent on mischief started to go towards where the turkeys were feeding; the old lady called to him to come back or she would give him a charge of buck shot; he started and ran; she up with the gun and was about to fire when Jim tripped her up, Dan took the gun and threw it into a ditch near by; we then drove on.

One mile from here we came to the twelve-mile forest of oak. We travelled until dark and were obliged to camp in the woods for the night; the night came on very dark and began to rain about seven and we were obliged to stand guard over our oxen to keep them together. Richard Fuller and three more were stationed around the cattle, thinking they would be the most trustworthy of any and the rest of us were sitting around the fire, when we heard something creeping up through the bushes and the first we knew a panther sprang within ten feet of us and gave one of the most unearthly screams that ever was heard; it made the hair stand up straight on our heads and in a moment more we heard an answering call far away in the forest. Richard Fuller ran and hid himself under a brush heap for safekeeping, which caused him much trouble afterwards. We were standing on each side of the cattle to keep them from breaking away again. Burt's and the Fullers on one side, Parker's and mine on the other, when Burt's gave a scream that made the cattle spring sideways quite over us. We picked ourselves up without getting hurt very much and we thought we would pay them off in their own coin, so we then gave a loud whoop and the cattle sprang back knocking down the Fuller's and Burt's and frightening them very much, besides being very wrathy; the cattle got away and spread out in the dark woods and it took all of us more than two hours to gath-

Chapter IV

er them up again and we finally came to the conclusion that it was better to chain the cattle up to trees, set a guard and turn in for the night.

About three o'clock in the morning we were awakened by the guard and they said they had heard a cry in the forest that sounded like a woman in distress; they had heard it four times within the last hour and they were very sure it must be some one in distress and thought we had better turn out and see what it was, so we all started except the guard and Fuller, he got under the blankets. We had gone about forty rods when we heard the cry and it seemed quite near now. Burt said, "Look out boys, it may not be a woman." "Woman or devil," says Dan, "I am going to see what it is." He had not taken more than ten steps when something shot from the branch of a tree and bore Dan to the ground. We all ran to help him and with our guns we beat him off, but we dared not fire for fear of hitting Dan. We beat him off none too quick, for Dan was badly scratched and torn as it was, and will carry the marks as long as he lives. We supposed it to be an Indian devil, a specie of cougar, a very unpleasant caller on such a dark night.

CHAPTER V

Still on the March — Platte River — Small Pox — Cholera — Missouri — A Fire — Hunting and Fishing — Camp on the Missouri — Among the Arapahoes — More Trouble with the Indians — Setting Guard — Fighting the Indians — The Dead and Wounded — Crossing the Little and Big Vermillion — Arrival on the Elk-Horn River — Fish and Game — A Prairie Dog Town — A Lonely Traveller — Etc., Etc., Etc.

We made up a large fire in the center of the camp, thinking it best to set up until morning. Parker began to tell a ghost story of rather a startling nature to those of a superstitious mind; every now and then Fuller would look over his shoulder into the dark forest, expecting a legion of devils to come and take him off bodily, but nothing happened until morning.

When it was light enough to see we hitched up and rolled on ten miles, and when we came out into the open country turned out and got breakfast. This day we travelled through a large wood with a good many wild turkeys and grey squirrels and we killed quite a lot of game. Through here the wild turkey is quite a large bird, I think them better eating than the tame ones, and some of them we get

Chapter V

would weigh fourteen pounds; they have a different flavor than the tame kind.

The next two days brought us to the small Platte River, six miles from St. Joseph, where we camped to recruit out cattle, which were rather tired after travelling several hundred miles through a wet, muddy country. The next day five of us went into the town to buy an outfit for the Plains; as we were going by a field we heard some jabbering, and we thought likely it was blacks; so Jim sang out, "Who is that?" Then a voice on the other side of the ditch answered, "this am Jim," and then they laughed. There was two of them, man and woman, and they were planting corn. We asked them if master whipped them often. "Yes," they said, "once and sometimes twice a day;" they liked him all the better for that, they said, and went on working. We went on into the town, where we found the small pox carrying the emigrants off in large numbers into the ground instead of to California, their original destination, the cholera was raging fearfully, and they were dying off by the hundreds; the authorities kept it very secret, planting them in the night.

This is a very lively place, and a great deal of trading is done with the numerous emigrant cattle; they buy provisions to last the months to cross the Plains; a large trade is also done in horses, mules and cattle. I think Missouri is the best farming country that I have yet seen. It is very rolling, and in some parts considerable hills may be seen. I observed large fields of corn standing four feet high. The State, as far as I have seen it, is well watered and wooded; all along the rivers the cottonwood tree is plenty and grows very large, and they take the place of the white pine of the Northern States.

As we were going out to camp, in passing a small house that appeared to be unoccupied, I was looking at a sign in the window when I observed smoke coming through the shingles, and in a few minutes the flames burst through the windows. We gave the alarm that started the people from their money thoughts to come to the rescue. There being no engine in town we got a line of buckets going for a long distance, but it soon got the upper hand over all our exertions and communicated with two other buildings. The wind that had until now been quite calm, began to rise, and the conflagration became general, spreading out in all directions. Some one suggested the use of gun powder; this was acted upon instanter and three kegs were brought from the nearest store; the next thing was how to place it where it might do the most advantage, some said place it on the first floor, others in the cellar. All this took time, and the fire had now become a mighty furnace, but they could only look on and wring their hands in despair as their homes were being swept away. The powder was placed, at last, and three deafening intonations were heard, at the same time the air was filled with the wreck of three large buildings, nearly a thousand people rushed out of the way of the debris and kept the fire from crossing this levelling by powder. The effect of the powder was wonderful, two of the buildings being completely levelled, in another about two thirds of it was blown away, we pulled it down with ropes and we said to the fire, "Thus far shalt thou go and no more," whereupon it burnt itself to sleep. Many buildings were destroyed by fire, others by powder, making twenty-one in all. This was a serious loss, they losing most nearly all of their household goods, their clothing as well. There were no lives lost, although some few were badly scorched.

As we could do nothing more we went back to camp pretty well tired out. The next day Barry's train came up and camped near us; this was the train we intended to travel with. For the next six days we went hunting and fishing, making spare yokes and anything we thought would be of use to us on the Plains. The next day old Burr, the Newfoundland dog, came dragging in a large grey wolf; they must have had quite a battle, for old Burr was pretty badly torn, his thick hair giving him the advantage. The wolf and Burr were about the same weight. Back in Iowa Burr nearly killed two calves, and would if Dan had not taken him off. Burr must have thought this a calf of a different stripe. Dan says he will go for an Indian every time.

On the 23rd of May we yoked up and rolled into town, and took our turn in crossing the river in the ferry boat, which we did about sunset, and camped on the right bank of the Missouri, in the Indian Territory. Our train consisted of sixteen wagons, one hundred and fifty head of cattle, thirty men, women and children, all told.

Chapter V

We now formed our wagons in a circle, with all hands in the center, and we set eight men on guard to look out for water thieves and land thieves; such as they are always in order wherever one may go. One of the guard having taken more firewater than was good for him, fell asleep at his post; some of the boys, on mischief bent, tied the sleeper down by the hair of his head. About day we heard him swearing at a supposed Indian; we heard him say, "Let me up, you doggone Injun; let my scalp alone, you doggone savage; help, doggone it, I shall lose my scalp, doggone the doggone Injuns." This rumpus raised the whole camp; Barry being commander-in-chief, gave them a lecture on discipline, which some of them needed very much; that man did not sleep on his guard again during the journey. The next morning having taken on six hundred pounds of bacon and six hundred of flour, we travelled eight miles over the worst road we have seen yet, dodging among the trees, over roots, and into deep holes, from which we came out shaking off the mud, and then down into another deeper yet; this was a forest of bass and cottonwood, the trees were large and quite straight. It was eight miles across this valley before we reached the high land or plain; here we camped until the next day to think of anything that we might have forgotten, for now we were fairly at sea, the next morning, after a good deal of trouble in separating each team. From here it is sixteen miles to the Mission, a small enclosure of ten acres or more; here a missionary stays to impose on the simplicity of the Indians, and drink firewater to keep their courage up.

The land appears to be good, very rolling, with now and then a small patch of timber; the road is bad in places; one of the teams got stuck and we were forced to unload. The opposite bank was very slippery with a kind of clay, which made it very hard to land. The Irishman and his wife, quite recently married, got nearly at the top when the lady's feet slipped from under her and they both fell and slid down into the muddy water below; but we soon got them out again, with some little addition. When they were landed high and dry we all gave three cheers that our exertions were crowned with success.

We now had left all civilization behind, no bridges or roads or public houses; the road had become a mere trail. In the vicinity of the Mission there was a few fields of corn and wheat, rye and oats, the labor is mostly done by the squaws, the men fight and hunt and they are a busy set when not on the war path. This is the Arapaho tribe, not very warlike, but very treacherous, and cannot be trusted. The next day at noon we saw several Indians some ways ahead and we motioned to them to get out of the trail; the cattle smelled them and would not advance. The Indians did not stir out of their tracks for some time. We urged the cattle along for some way when the whole train stampeded and ran nearly a mile, smashing one wheel into kindling wood. This accident caused us to turn out and camp on the left bank of the Little Blue River. There we formed the wagons in a half circle for our better defense in case of an attack by the Indians that began to come around quite plenty. Almost all trades were represented in our company and they soon got materials for a new wheel and late in the afternoon they had it well advanced. I was standing looking on to see the novel way they took to set the tire, when all at once a big Indian put his arms around me from behind and gave me such a jerking I did not know for a moment which end I was on; he was a powerful fellow, but did not know how to lay his strength out to advantage. I soon drew my hands out and twisted around so that I faced him, then I brought that old Indian down with a squall like a big pumpkin and held him there, when the rest of the boys came and said I must let him up as the Indians were coming to attack us. I let him get up and away he ran to his tribe. Said I, "Boys, we must get our guns and drive them back; they mean mischief." So we forced them back in a half circle and five men kept them there with loaded guns. At this time there was more than a hundred, nearly all of them large men. It seems that this big savage was their bully, and if he had thrown me they would have attacked us instanter. As I walked along in front of them they would point at me and give a grunt as much as to say "Him bad medicine;" some one gave them a chunk of pork, with a string tied through it, and it was quite laughable to see them hold it up and grunt; they did not know what to make of it. Pretty soon one of them went and threw it into the brush as bad medicine, no doubt.

Chapter V

About sundown they all went away; "Good riddance, bad rubbish," we said, but we had not seen the last of them. At dark we got the cattle up and the sergeant placed eight men on guard, with strict injunction to keep their eyes open tight for any red skin that might be lurking about. Two men were on guard in front of the wagons, every one of us looked to the priming of our guns and then lay down to get some rest, for we knew not what the morrow might bring forth. About ten o'clock the cattle broke away; the noise of their feet, as we lay on the ground, sounded like distant thunder; we all ran out expecting the Indians had come, but none could we see. We got the cattle together once more and one of the guards was run over and considerably hurt.

At midnight the guard was changed; about three o'clock Barry called us all up and said the Indians might attack us at any moment; he then gave us some general rules to go by, but we must act according to circumstances whatever they might be. Dan and I went to reconnoiter to the left of our marque, while Sam and Joe went to the right. As I was peering through the darkness Dan fired, then the other two men fired at the right; the Indians were now upon us in large numbers with horrid yells, but they were taken aback when they found us prepared to receive them; even Fuller fought like a tiger. The main attack came from the back of the wagons. I pinned two that were crawling under a wagon; Jim not having a gun took his frying pan and laid about him so well that he laid out six; this was doing better than any of us. In less than twenty minutes the Indians had retreated, leaving six carcasses on the ground, ten more badly wounded; four of our own party received wounds from arrows and spears. Jim thought we had better dispatch what Indians we had on hand as there would be plenty more before we got through, but we concluded to dress their wounds and leave them there. At first we feared the arrows had been poisoned, but they were not, although the wounds they made were very painful; in pulling them out some flesh came with them.

At daylight we drove the cattle down where there was plenty of grass, and as soon as they had filled themselves we hitched up and every man that could carry a gun marched on each side of the train.

We had not gone more than two miles when we saw two hundred Indians, two on a pony dressed in war paint, with their spears, bows and arrows. They saw at once that we were ready to receive them and therefore made no demonstration, but went by as hard as they could go.

We travelled sixteen miles this day and camped where there was plenty of grass and we kept a bright lookout for Indians, but none came around that night. The next day we crossed the Little Vermillion, a very pretty stream with plenty of fish, some very large catfish we saw in the deeper pools. The grass all along the banks is good, also cottonwood and slippery elm; this we peeled off and eat in large quantities, it being a rarity to most of us in a green state, and I found it much better than in a dry condition. The land appears the best I have yet seen; it is rolling like the waves of the ocean as far as the eye can extend. The next day we crossed the Big Vermillion, with a swift current running over white stones and flat rocks as clear as crystal, the banks covered with large cottonwood trees. We saw a few currant bushes and a species of cowslip growing near the margin of the stream. The Irishman's wife took off her stockings and shoes and waded the river, having got behind. I thought the current would upset the lady, but she being quite weighty she crossed with flying colors. When she arrived on the other shore the boys gave a shout that rang far and near, which made her rather vexed. "If you are laughing at me, you spalpeens," she said, "I will be after learning you better manners," shaking her shoes and stockings at them.

About this time Fuller became very homesick, saying he wished he was at home with his wife and children. I think the man would have given all he had if he could have gone back at this time. We told him we did not believe that they would expect him, if he should. He said he was never so far away from home before, and was afraid he should never return again alive.

The weather now being quite pleasant three of the ladies of our train came out in bloomer costume and the younger ones looked quite nice in short clothes; they were great walkers and could get on much better in this rig. Here we found six men camped on the bank, with a handcart, going to California on their own hook. Here the

Chapter V

cholera begins to show its enmity to the human race. The next day we passed a number of new graves, also a number of teams returning back; they had lost so many from cholera that they were not able to proceed.

The next two days we travelled forty miles and camped on the Elk-Horn river, a bright stream some sixty feet wide, running quite fast.

All these streams seem to have plenty of fish, the catfish predominating. We see many deer and antelope scampering over the hills. I have a double barrel gun, one a shot barrel, the other a rifle barrel. I shot something almost every day; the game seems quite shy. Dan came in today with a fine doe. I have been trying to get a shot at an antelope but have not succeeded as yet; we can get plenty of prairie hens. Off a little way on the Plain is a prairie dog town, with every now and then a sentinel perched on a clod of earth to give warning of coming danger. As we came near the warning would be given and up would pop hundreds of heads. Where they live the ground is all honeycombed with their underground roadways and one falls through at every step. Here old Burr had fun enough for some time trying to catch the little scamps.

We are now two hundred miles west of St. Joseph. To day a man passed us at a quick walk with an umbrella over his head and a pack on his back containing his blankets and provisions, bound for the land of gold, nearly three thousand miles away. What will man not do for the charmer gold!

CHAPTER VI

The Packer — The Tornado — Attack by Indians — The Pursuit — The Fight — The Rescue — The Killed and Wounded — Return to Camp — Fort Kearney — In the Pawnee Country — The Storm — Buffalo Antelope, and Deer — The Old Bull — Crossing the South Fork of the Platte — Arrival at a Trading Post — French Canadians — The Sioux Natives —Crossing the "Glorious Fourth" — Etc., Etc., Etc.

The next day we came up with the packer. He was nearly worn out, his feet all bandaged and he was about used up. As we put his baggage on our team and carried it for him for two days, when towards night, about two hours before sunset, thick, heavy storm clouds rolled up from the northeast. The darkness came on very sudden and we encamped as soon as possible. I have never known the darkness come on so fast before, Barry said we must make ready for a tornado. The tents were pitched and braced as well as circumstances would permit, we chained our sixteen wagons together and got the cattle under the lee of some cottonwood trees. In a short time the wind began to rise, coming from the south, but soon changed to the northeast; it blew a gale and it seemed as though we

Chapter VI

could hear the evil spirits screaming in the upper air. About midnight the roar of the tornado was terrific; it lifted and twisted the entire sixteen wagons into a confused heap, the teams were pressed down flat as a pancake and their contents lifted, twisted and thrown together, and it was difficult to tell who was which, the heavens were one blazing flame of electric light, and it seemed as though the crack of doom was at hand; the rest of the tempest seemed to last forever, although it was over in two hours, the stars came out and all was calm as before. I held an umbrella in front of the wagon to keep out the storm, but a gust of wind took it out of my hand and it was gone; at the same time a gun was fired. Fuller and three more stood on guard that night, and Fuller said he shot at a big black wolf. The next morning I found my umbrella one and a half miles from camp, at the junction of the Independence road, with a bullet hole in it; it was so badly smashed it was unfit for use. I showed Fuller the bullet hole and he turned away with a sorrowful look; not a dry thread of clothes could be found in camp that morning. The little packer looked like a drowned rat and this took away that courage that had sustained him thus far, and when we hitched up to proceed on our journey he turned his face towards his distant home, two hundred and fifty miles distant though in an enemy's country, and his scalp no doubt hangs in a corner of some Indian lodge.

The next day we passed by fifty graves—the effects of that remorseless disease, cholera. The atmosphere seemed heavy with miasma, and we all felt more and more unwell. One trouble was the dead were not buried deep enough; the wolves and other night prowlers had dug them out, and in some cases the corpses were exposed. It did seem strange that they should plant them so near the trail.

Today we met nine teams in one train turning back; four wagons had started with eighteen, and were returning with six; twelve had been taken; this was fearful. We hurried by three fresh mounds with all dispatch possible.

The land through here is quite level as far as the eye can extend. A large herd of deer and antelope are in sight most of the time. Two of the boys on horseback gave chase to some deer, and it was quite an exciting scene as they scampered over the Plain, the deer keeping along way in advance. Today we met two men returning at a rapid walk with their guns; they said they belonged to four wagons with nine others, and while encamped the Indians came upon them and they fought as long as they could stand up, many being killed and wounded, the rest then were carried away captive and their cattle driven away, and they felt bad, as any one would under the circumstances; they asked us to go with them and try and get them back; this we consented to do, for they said they were not more than five miles away. The train was ordered to proceed four miles and camp; ten men well armed were selected to go with the two men; Jim wanted to go with his frying pan. I told him if we were both killed the company would be without a cook, and as I had a double barrel gun I had better go, that would do for both of us. In ten minutes we were off on the double quick. At about noon we thought we had passed over ten miles and we did not like to leave our train too far away, as we knew not how many Indians there might be prowling around.

We went on two miles further and came to a small valley; here we saw the four wagons and six lodges of Indians; the guides said that was their train, they knew. The next thing was how to come upon them and so take them by surprise; if we could wait until night we might capture them without much loss. Time was valuable and we felt anxious in regard to our own people; drawing out ten men had left them quite weak, but we concluded to wait until dark before making further advance. As near as our two guides could tell they had been attacked by nearly sixty Indians, but from the number of lodges I should say about thirty. The time passed slow until we should go for them; it came at last; one of our men, a little wiry man, was sent forward to reconnoiter the Indian camp; the rest of us creeping up as near as possible. In twenty minutes our guide returned and said the Indians were carousing over their late victory and now would be a good time to go for them. Our two guides were just spoiling for the fight; they being the most interested party we let them go ahead; four of us came up behind the outer lodges; we lifted up the edge and looked in, and there lay bound two of their men and we soon released them; they said the two women and three

Chapter VI

children were in the third tent. There was a sentinel before the tent and he was soon dispatched. No firearms having been used up to this time the Indians had not been alarmed, but as the savage fell he cried out; this brought the Indians out and we fell upon them tooth and nail. The fight did not last more than ten minutes, but it was lively work while it did last. The Indians being taken by surprise soon gave way at all points, and we were masters of the situation. We found we had lost no men and only two were wounded, one lay insensible on the ground, having been struck down with a knotted war club; he came to after a while and was able to sit up. After a time six were sent to hunt up the cattle and in about an hour they came back with all of them, except one ox that they found had been killed and partly eaten.

Having had nothing to eat since morning we made a fire and cooked a good square meal and this made us feel better. We now yoked up the cattle and made preparations to return, as the Indians might rally and give us more trouble. The two wounded men were placed in the wagons, also the women and children; we also cut off the best of the ox and stowed it away for future use. It was now near midnight as we judged from the position of the yardstick in heavens, and we took our course so we might strike the trail a little to the West of where we started in the morning. A little after daylight we came upon the trail and found from signs that we were ahead of our train. We took the back track and in a mile we reached our own camp, where they had given us up as lost, as we did not return at night; they had seen no Indians since we left them in the morning. Jim was very glad to see me come back, and he said he had slept with his hand on his frying pan all night. Our two wounded men were doing well and were about in three days. We camped over one day as we had had no sleep the night before.

The next day we came up where the fight the day before had been, and there lay parts of two white men and five Indians; we planted them in two separate graves. The scene was a very sad one to the friends and near relatives; a chapter was read from the New Testament and the graves were filled in and we passed on our way.

Three days journey from here we came to Fort Kearney, on the

Platte River, three hundred miles from St. Joseph. The land appears to be very poor and barren of all vegetation, nothing growing but a little stunted grass and a dwarf willow. There being no wood we were obliged to burn buffalo chips; these lay in great numbers on the ground, and with a spade we cut two small trenches in the ground, some six inches wide and eight inches deep, in the form of a star, placed the chips in these trenches, set our kettles over them, and in this way we cooked very well. The chips make a hot fire, giving off quite a pleasant smell; this was all the fuel we had for four hundred miles.

Fort Kearney is a walled enclosure built of adobe brick, hardened in the sun; they are two feet by three feet in thickness, the wall is eight feet high, and about one hundred and fifty men are stationed here at this time; they only dared to go about twenty rods from the fort, for their scalps were in such good demand.

The valley, or plain, here is about two miles wide; most of the way for seven hundred miles the river at the Fort is a mile wide, with a moving quicksand. We are now in the Pawnee nation, a very numerous and warlike tribe, and are large and well made men; they have good horses and can ride to perfection, and when on the warpath two of them ride on a pony. I have seen quite a number of Mexican saddles taken in their raids on Mexico, and I have no doubt there is nothing they like better or will give more for, than a Mexican scalp; the reason why I cannot tell, unless it is they are thick settled. I have seen the squaws picking the vermin off and eating them as fast as found, and without any sauce to go with them.

The third day from this we found the grass very scarce, and at night we went down into a second valley below where the grass was rather better near the river. About the middle of the afternoon it clouded up, and soon after camping it began to rain. The wind soon got its back up and the tornado was dancing a jig with Beelzebub in watercolor; the fountains of the great deep were pouring their surplus waters upon us. Heaven's artillery blazed in all its mighty grandeur and man seemed but a small affair cringing beneath all this rattle bang and crash of the warring elements.

About midnight the river overflowed its banks and the valley became untenable; our cattle had become so frightened by the noise of the tempest that they had fled away some time before, and the darkness being intense we were unable to find them until noon the next day, some five miles down the river in a wood; so we run the wagons up on higher ground by hand; this required some two hours hard labor. Soon after the storm had passed and the stars were shining as bright as ever. At daylight we thought of breakfast; our Buffalo chips were all wet so we went to the distant hills, three miles away, and found a few dwarf cedars, and with these we got a late breakfast of venison and bacon.

Buffalo, antelope and deer are very plenty all through this section of country. The next day we camped over until Monday morning. Saturday morning six of us started off early in quest of buffalo, and after going five miles we came to a place where we could look down into a valley; there we saw a sight that we had not yet seen before. There, within a mile of us, unconscious of any danger, were more than five thousand buffalo; we were spell bound at the sight, and for some time watched their motions. On the outside of the heard was an old bull, as sentinel; every little while he would raise his head and sniff the air. Some dozen or more wolves were watching them some few rods off. The next thing was to get to the leeward of them and then work up to them within rifle range, and this we did after a time. Dan had a very heavy rifle, carrying about sixty to the pound. Each one of us singled out a cow, except Dan, and he said he must have the old bull. At a given signal we all blazed away at the same instant; three cows were seen to fall, but the old bull came straight for us. We loaded as quick as we could, but before were ready we were obliged to "git up and git."

This was a race worth looking at; he charged by three of us and others poured in their fire as he went by, and he dropped just as he was about to give Thomas a lift. Here were three cows and a bull, the rest of the herd scamped away. The next thing was to build a fire, for there was plenty of fuel in the shape of buffalo chips; here was tenderloin steak in abundance, and we made a good square meal, then cut off what we could carry and started on our return. I think I never in all my life enjoyed any meat as I did this; it was very tender and juicy, more so than tame cattle, and should say they would weigh from six to eight hundred pounds each. We arrived about dark, our packs being quite welcome. That night the smell of beef went through the camp generally, and was accepted as a fact.

Four days travel and we crossed the south fork of the Platte. At this place the river is a mile wide, from three to six feet deep. We came up to the crossing place about three in the afternoon, and two men on horses went to examine the ford, one above and one below. There were a good many places their horses had to swim and we concluded to wait until morning. As the river is constantly changing, the water is quite thick with sand and the current being very swift it makes it a bad spot to get over.

About eight the next morning we raised our wagon bodies up by placing buffalo skulls under them to keep our provisions dry, if possible. This was very important, as there was no port of entry where we could lay in a supply for twenty-five hundred miles. We hitched on eight yoke of oxen to each wagon so the forward cattle would be where their feet would touch bottom; while the others were swimming we were obliged to have a man to each yoke of oxen that we might keep them moving, for the instant they stopped they would begin to settle down into the sand. This was a hard pull, the current was very swift and would nearly take us off our feet. One driver was swept down against the chain, and if it had not been for that he would have been lost. We made two trips across with each team, with very good luck; four other teams took the upper ford and got their provisions wet and came very near being drowned. Jim said he had a good mind to float across in his frying pan. The water was quite cold and were pretty well chilled when we got through. The day was quite pleasant and our things were spread out in the sun and soon dried. Here we left our buffalo skulls for the use of those on the return, and so they answer a good purpose.

The next morning we rolled on fourteen miles through a fine country as any we could wish to see. Our camping ground would be a good site for a town; the location is almost perfect, and the land produces large plants that would make good forage. Timber is scarce, but now and then a small patch can be seen in the distance.

Chapter VI

The next day brought us to Ranbedoe's trading post. He is located among the hills and trades with the Indians. They bring in their poultry and in exchange he gives them guns, ammunition, traps, blankets and large quantities of firewater. He had several squaws at work making moccasins, quite prettily adorned with several colored beads. Our boys bought several pairs, they being light to travel in over the prickly pear, which covers the ground for several hundred miles. Rubedough [sic] says he sends two trains a year to the States, and we met one of his trains two days back, twelve wagons, each wagon drawn by thirteen yoke of oxen; the drivers, twelve in number, were French Canadians, and each load is piled up high like a load of hay; they intend to carry about five tons to a wagon. The wheels to these wagons are a wonder of themselves; the fellows are six inches wide and eight inches deep; the body is made watertight to cross the rivers. When they camp at night they form their wagons into a hollow square, and in this, their fort, the cattle are herded at night. As every man must drive his team all day, they must sleep at night.

We are now in the Sioux nation. They are a very savage looking tribe, and have the appearance of having plenty to eat, which cannot always be said of white folks in civilized life.

Six days travel brought us to Fort Sareny. We left the trail for a mile and turned into a nice valley containing some thousand acres or more, where the grass was three feet high. Here the cattle luxuriated to their hearts' content for two days.

The next day was the "glorious Fourth" and we celebrated our Independence by raising two blankets on a pole and firing twenty-six guns. There was one other train camped about a half mile up the valley, and they also had a flag up and made considerable noise. About the middle of the forenoon they sent an ambassador with full power to invite our company to a noon performance. This was an item in the day's pleasure we had not looked forward to. Having heard there were several ladies there we had to fix up as well as we could; this brought out our Bowie knives to shave with, and what they did not cut off they pulled out by the roots; this had a tendency to give our faces some color which some of us did not have.

CHAPTER VII

A New Surprise — The Wedding — The Ball — "Miss Big Wolf" — Court House Rock — Chimney Rock — Castle Rock — Crossing the North Fork of the Platte — Independence Rock — The Sweet Water — The Devil's Gate—Pacific Springs — A Hail Storm — Attacked by Wolves — A Sad Accident — Green River — Parting Company — Salt Lake Mountain — A Raid on the Cattle — The Fight — "Old Burr" Again — A Prisoner — The Punishment — Etc., Etc., Etc.

We had four ladies in our train, and they dressed in bloomer costume with ribbons flying in the breeze. At the top of the snare drum twenty-two of us in a line abreast, with fife and drum, marched to the tune of "Yankee Doodle," with the ladies in the center swinging their kerchiefs of many colors that carried a perfume on the morning air, and thus we marched to the festive camp where we were received with genuine pleasure. A large pavilion had been fitted up for the occasion, by the use of tents and wagon covers, so there was room for all.

We were now taken by surprise, for a lady and gent stepped in the center, then another with a book in his hand. We began now to

Chapter VII

smell a mice; the man in black now told them to join hands, which they did with much pleasure, from the looks of a blushing bride; the clergy man then proceeded with the marriage rite, and they two were made one. After kissing the blushing bride all around, with some confection and genuine invitation to come to the ball in the evening, so thanking them for the most pleasure we had received we returned in the same order as we came.

Three of our hunters had gone out after deer and had brought in two large bucks; one of these we sent to the friendly camp with our compliments. The time was now occupied with various games until the hour of the entertainment, 7 o'clock, when we started in full force, except the guard over the cattle. Soon after we arrived the ball was opened by the groom and bride taking their places at the head for a country dance first and third couples balance; they had two fiddles and a clarinet, and our fifer and drummer as assistants. There was room for two cotillions on the boards, and where they obtained them I could not tell. At 11 o'clock the party broke up and "We went home with the gals in the morning," as the song goes.

The next morning early we rolled on. Just before noon we met a tribe of Sioux Indians; the chief had his daughter, "Me Big Wolf," with him, and she was the prettiest Indian girl I had ever seen; she was dressed in bloomer costume made of silk and nearly covered with many colored beads. She had a nice sidesaddle and the pony was milk white, and she sat on the pony as though she grew there. They went by without even saying, "How do you do, sir?"

In the afternoon we came to "Court House Rock;" it stands one mile from the river on a ridge of the hills, and at a distance it has the appearance of a courthouse with a cupola on the top. It is one hundred feet square at the base and about ninety feet high, with uniform steps from the bottom to the top, so one can ascend to the top where we have a splendid view over the vast plain below.

Ten miles further on is "Chimney Rock." This rock is about three hundred feet high composed of fine sand stone; this is about two hundred feet square at the base. The chimney is about forty feet square at the place where the chimney begins, and then runs up one hundred and fifty or more feet in height, where it tapers to four feet, and we could go up some two hundred feet. This was a fine view, and away in the distance could be seen large herds of buffalo, deer and antelope; not a bush or tree could be seen in the hundred thousand acres in sight.

Twelve miles further on we came to "Castle Rock." This is about ninety feet high, perfectly level on top, and covers some twenty acres, with a parapet ten feet deep on three sides. Near the edge lay some immense stones, and six of us went on the top with a crowbar and dislodged a stone that would weigh, I should think, more than a hundred tons. This more than paid us for our trouble to see them go crashing down; when they struck they would burst with a loud report and roll out into the plain below.

We now had twelve miles of nice travelling, with fine bracing air that gave us new courage to go on. This would make a fine agricultural country, for the land seems to be excellent, producing a grass very nutritious by the action it had on our cattle.

The next day we came to the place where we must cross the north fork of the Platte. There was a large train of Missourians camped here ready to cross. The next day we hired their wagon box to cross in. The cattle were got over that afternoon and we drove them in, but could not for a long time make them swim over. Three horsemen were in the water over an hour. The river is deep and swift. Finally, one ox started across, then they all followed, and were over. Two extra men were sent over to guard them through the night. Now comes the tug of war to get the wagons and freight across. We caulked up the old wagon box, and after taking out the freight rolled it on board and started, one on each side to row and one to steer. We had pulled but two strokes when the whole thing capsized in four feet of water. It was lucky we were not in deep water, if we had been the wagon would have been lost, as well as myself, as I could not swim. Jim said he would have bailed the river out with his frying pan, but he would have had me out. We got the wagon out and took off the wheels; they did the mischief by catching the current; we placed the wheels in the bottom of the box, and the rest on top, and started over again and arrived on the other shore without further accident, the current taking us down nearly a quarter mile,

Chapter VII

unload, then draw the box up again and start across. This work lasted until after sunrise. When we changed our clothes for dry ones, we had a good breakfast, with hot coffee, and then turned in until noon, when we rolled on over the hills six miles and camped.

Three days travel from here we came to "Independence Rock," a boulder sitting on top of the ground nearly six hundred feet square. I should judge it to be excellent granite. From here it is forty-three miles to the South Pass in the Rocky Mountains.

The next two days brought us to the "Sweet Water," a beautiful stream full of mountain trout. These fish are excellent and I could eat one more after being full. One day we crossed the stream four times; it is quite deep and sometimes water came into the wagon box. Jim got behind again and had to wade through, not very pleasant, as the water is from the melting snows of the Rocky Mountains, twenty miles away. We had been ascending for the last seven hundred miles and were pretty well up among the rocks. In the afternoon we came to a place where the rocks were very steep, and we had to double up our teams in order to draw the wagons up. For the last five hours we had travelled on solid rock. About sunset we came to some grass where we camped for the night. The next day snow lay near the train and snow balling was the order; the air here is cold and bracing, old age I don't think has any camp in this region; we all seemed to brace up under this life giving climate.

The next day, at noon, we passed through the "Devil's Gate" and camped for noon; this is a narrow passage not more than twenty feet wide, the rocks on each side are perpendicular and run up one hundred feet. This is the only place the mountains can be crossed for a hundred and fifty miles. The Sweet Water passes between the "Gate" and is cold and clear as crystal. In the afternoon we travelled seven miles and camped for two days to recruit the cattle and wash and mend our clothes. There we caught trout in abundance, and a number of us went out after game; we looked for bears but saw none, nor game of any kind. This is a dreary and desolate country; the great crop of this section is snow and ice.

Seventy miles from here we came to "Pacific Springs," [perhaps Pacific Creek now] the dividing ridge between the Atlantic and

Pacific oceans; here the water runs towards the west; the land around the springs lay on the water and one can shake acres of it. Our cattle were very dry when we arrived here, and several got in and we had hard work to get them out. Half a mile below the Spring, we dug holes, and in six inches we came to solid ice; it seems the snow and ice never melts here.

The second day from here just as we had camped there came up a tremendous hail storm and it was very fortunate we had camped, for the hailstones, some of them were as large as hen's eggs; if the cattle had been hitched to the wagons they would have ran and smashed them all to kindling wood. The cattle were sore for ten days afterwards. In gulleys where the hailstones had washed down they were four feet deep.

From here it is twenty miles to the "Big Sandy" [probably Little Sandy]. We carried but little water to drink and soon was out. We arrived at Big Sandy about dark and found the stream dry as a contribution box. At springtime this was a sad disappointment, but we were forced to camp; the cattle could proceed no further that night. This is a sandy and barren waste made to hold the world together only. We set a guard, ate a few mouthfuls, and turned in.

About eleven o'clock we were awakened by hearing a shot, then another, then we heard the cattle bellow; this was unusual, and we all ran out with our guns, which we always kept loaded over night. We ran down to the cattle, for the guard was having their hands full; when we got there we had our hands full also; a pack of grey wolves had come down upon them before the guard was aware of it, and so took them by surprise. We now opened fire on the brutes and killed lots of them. Jim was there with his frying pan and smashed them right and left.

Jim and I were together at one time, and lucky it was, for a big wolf jumped on to Jim's back and fastened his teeth in his neck. Jim gave an awful yell, and as soon as I could see what was the matter I gave the wolf a punch with my gun barrel that it nearly went through the brute, and he rolled over dead; one tooth had passed through a cord and three had made flesh wounds; the cord being injured made his neck stiff. For some time Jim said I saved his life,

Chapter VII

but I don't know; I think he would have got up and shook him off.

It was quite fortunate the cattle huddled together or we should have lost quite a number; two were so badly torn and we were obliged to kill them; in twenty minutes we had driven them off, but they left twelve of their number on the field of battle. We now built fires around the cattle, set a double guard, and then went to camp. I put some hot drops on Jim's neck to keep the swelling down, and he said it pained badly; it kept him awake the rest of the night. The guard said the wolves came near enough to see their eyeballs, that looked so fiery, but made no attack; one man was bitten in the hand, but not badly.

The next morning we found several of the oxen were badly torn; we sewed them up as well as we could and they did very well. Of the two we had to kill, we cut off the best parts of them and jerked it for future use. We not having had any water for twenty-four hours, as soon as it was day we moved on eight miles to Little Sandy [probably Big Sandy], where we found a little water, then went on to Millet Spring and camped for the night. From here it's a gradual descent for one hundred miles [probably fifty miles] to Green River.

The next day we travelled eighteen miles and camped in a small grove of cottonwood until Monday morning. A family in Barry's train, of four members, by the name of Stetson, were looking on to see their oldest son of nineteen years draw a charge from a pistol, when it went off, the ball passing through his breast, and he lived but ten minutes; this was very sad, for he was a very promising young man and it was a hard blow for his parents. They had left comfort and a good home that he might try his fortune in a new land. Our three wagons had camped apart the day before; as we wished to travel on a little different principle. They came and notified us and we went and dug the grave, and after reading a chapter from the New Testament we laid him in his lonely grave, and as the clods of earth fell upon the rude box his mother could stand no more and was kindly taken away. We now filled in the grave, piling a large quantity of stones on the ground that the remorseless grey wolf could not disturb the remains.

We found water scarce, and grass also, all the way from here to

In Search of Gold

Green River. This is a beautiful stream, some fifty yards wide, with a swift current, clear and very cold. The stream is bordered with a growth of cottonwood and bass. Our three wagons crossed in the ferry, Barry's train went down the river half a mile and crossed there; we went down to see them. They placed a quantity of stones in their wagons to keep them down so that the current might not sweep them away; they took their course in a slant down the river and I expected every minute to see them swept away. The drivers were lifted off their feet but hung on to the yoke, and they all got across safely. From here they took the trail to the north that leads to Oregon, and I have never seen them since.

Our three wagons took the southwest to Salt Lake and California. From here to Salt Lake is one hundred and fifty miles; there being only six of us, each was pledged to stand guard three nights in the week. It is here that the Black Feet Indians flourish, and are pretty good for taking scalps. For eighty miles the land is poor and barren of grass and water; except at long intervals, and this was a hard tramp for the cattle, their feet had become sore and we threw them and shod them with leather, using copper tacks; they would stay on for two hundred miles or more, according as the travelling might be.

We now travelled through a canyon for six days, the scenery varying but little; the weather being very warm we travelled slow. In ten days from Green River we came to the Salt Lake Mountain; the last day's travel we had found the service berries very plenty; they grew in clusters and are a very nice fruit; there were bunches that were all ripe, others were part green and the berries are a little larger than the high blueberry, of a purple color. For two days travel the berries were in abundance; this is all the fruit we saw for three thousand miles and we enjoyed them greatly.

The next morning early we started up the ascent; this was a hard pull, and every little distance we had to double our teams to get over steep places. At night we had made four miles and camped on the top of the highest point of the pass. The next day we travelled seventeen miles and camped on a plateau of some two acres in extent and here we had a view of the great Salk Lake and its beautiful val-

Chapter VII

ley. One other wagon and four men camped along side of us and one of their men and two of ours stood guard that night. As we had heard hard stories about the Mormons we kept a strict watch. At twelve o'clock, midnight, it was my watch. I came out on time and found the guard sound asleep and the cattle gone. I alarmed the camp, and some started one way and some another, I started down the trail; it was bright moonlight and I got down on my knees and examined the trail and found they were going towards the valley; I also made out the print of a horse's foot, and also a dog's footprint. I thought it must be old Burr, as I had seen his track so many times and I hurried on. Pretty soon I heard some one coming behind and up came Jim with his frying pan, saying, "You don't go without me." We now hurried on as fast as we could and in about half an hour as we came to a bend of the trail, we saw two horsemen driving the cattle along as fast as they could make them go, and old Burr following them. Jim and I came up within twenty rods, when I sung out, "Surrender, or you are dead men!" One of them fired and the ball whistled by my head, but did not stop to take toll. I then opened fire but missed the man, but brought down the horse. The other horseman charged down upon us and I gave him a charge of buckshot, when he turned and fled, giving some heart-rendering yells; the buckshot was more than he expected; the other one had charged on foot, but Jim had flattened him out with his frying pan. By this time two more of the boys came up and we now bound our prisoner, while others got around the cattle and started back to camp, old Burr was helping to drive the horse which was still kicking in the brush, and Jim drew his knife across his throat to put him out of misery. In about an hour we arrived at camp all right, with our prisoner, who was quite sulky, with five black spots on his skin. We rubbed the wounds with salt and hot-drops and this treatment made him think of the hot place down below.

Now the cause of all this trouble and the narrow chance we had of losing all our cattle must be brought out for punishment. He belonged to our new acquaintances of the night before, Lampit was his name, and his companions said he must be punished for such careless disregard of our lives; he said there was no law there and he should not submit, but he had not more than spoken the last word when one of his own companions tripped him up. He was now held and tied and thrown on his face, and one of our men was appointed to use the ropes, and Sanders did his duty if he ever did it before, for the loss of our cattle would have meant death to us all; so he laid the rope's end on until the miscreant sang out for quarters; but Sanders' blood was up and he laid on until we said enough. He was then let go but was not trusted afterwards. It was now near day, and all being pretty thoroughly waked up, we concluded to get breakfast and go on.

CHAPTER VIII

The City of the Mormons — Grasshoppers — Cattle, Horses and Sheep — A Mormon Interviewed — Brigham as a Preacher — The Valley — Bear River — Arrive at the Spring — A Fight with Indians — The Wounded and Slain — The Humboldt River — Etc., Etc., Etc.

We now let our prisoner go under the promise of receiving death at our hands if he ever came in to the valley again, and he started back towards Green River. We knew if we allowed him to report to Young we should be set upon by the whole Mormon tribe. The prisoner said he was sent into the hills for that purpose. From here it is six miles to Bear River, where we arrived about ten in the forenoon. This is quite a deep stream, some sixty feet wide, bordered by a dense growth of wood, and a good place for bears, no doubt. From here it is seven miles [looks like forty miles] to the city, where we arrived in the afternoon and drove up Emigrant Street and into a yard where another train from Illinois was camped. We now were obliged to buy corn and hay, as we could not turn our cattle out on the common, for if we did we should lose them, as everything that is not well guarded is gobbled up by these people.

In Search of Gold

The city is laid out in a square, the streets running parallel to each other, and each street has a stream of clear mountain water running through it, also a row of shade trees on each side of the street; this arrangement made the city very pleasant to live in. Each cottage has two acres of land in front of it, and when you have seen one you have seen them all, they being built after one pattern. The land is excellent, throwing our Western land all into the shade. There was a field of wheat that was being cut. The men had gone to dinner and their cradles were laying idle, and our boys took hold and began to swing them through the grain; they found it something more than they had been used to, in fact it was all they could do, and soon gave it up. The grain stood four feet and a half high, and all their crops looked splendid; the kernel of the wheat is much larger than that of Illinois. Most of their land is irrigated on a systemized plan from the water of the melting snows on the mountains. The lake covers a large area, but seems not very deep; it is very salt, and in fact there is an incrustation of salt all around the edge of the water.

At this time the dead grasshoppers lay two inches thick, and a rod wide, all around the margin of the Lake. In some parts of the valley they had destroyed every green thing and the inhabitants had turned out en masse and driven them in the Lake and there they remained intact, pickled by salt.

They have large herds of cattle, horses and sheep. I saw no orchards of any kind; perhaps their winters are too cold, and they tell me the snows become very deep before spring, and the cold intense and very steady through the winter.

I had an opportunity to see a good many handsome ladies on the street; they dress very rich and mostly in silks. The females are the larger part of the inhabitants. What a splendid place to live, say I.

Young is now building an immense temple, and four hundred artisans are at work; it is being built of gray marble, of which they have a large quarry to draw from. They have nearly all the minerals that they require for every purpose. All their groceries cost them dear as they must be transported over land from the States by large wagon trains drawn by mules and oxen. The inhabitants, they told me, at this time were nearly nine thousand, four thousand males and five thousand females.

There was a Mormon in the yard where we camped, and we asked him how many wives he had; he said three. "Why don't you have more?" "Three is all I can support." Each one has wives according as he has means for their support. He said none had over fifteen, except the head of the church, and he had nearly fifty, but keeps only one with him. They said their husbands made them earn their own living. Several came into the yard to wash for the emigrants, and this required a good deal of soap, having put by our washing for four months.

They held a meeting one afternoon in the church, and this friendly Mormon told us we had better go up and hear what was said. Jim and I went; we stopped on the porch, the door was open and we could hear very well what was said. The church was well filled, mostly men. Brigham was the first speaker. He said, "My friends, I had a vision last night, and I saw Joe Smith as plain as I see you. He said, 'Brigham, you are doing just right. Yours is the only religion that is worth a d—n.'" At this point Jim snickered and a man came out; he said nothing but gave us a powerful look and went back. Brigham then went on to say, "The Gentiles were a stink and an abomination and should not dwell amongst them. Gird on the sword of Gideon and slay right and left." We stopped to hear no more, not that we were afraid of being converted unto their faith, but, as Jim said, of being slain.

We sold one wagon here, and I now bought some cloth to make a tent, as the one we had was rather close quarters. Jim and I occupied this ourselves the rest of the way of twelve hundred miles.

The next day, the fifth we had stopped here, we rolled out fifteen miles to a blacksmith's shop, had our tires on our wagons set, and got the oxen shod, for the rest of the journey of twelve hundred miles is a hard road to travel. The next day we started on and joined the Illinois train of six wagons, for it was not safe to travel alone. Our course lay up the valley, near the base of the mountains. We had a fine view of their system of irrigation. The Valley has a gentle slope to the Lake, giving them a chance to cultivate nearly the whole valley. The water is conducted from the gulch to a ditch running along the base of the mountains; it is then let down into smaller ditches and then divided and sub-divided until the land is all covered with little rivulets. The land is all laid out in sections, one above another, so that one man has the water today, and another at night.

The Valley is settled all the way, a distance of ninety miles, the best land I ever saw. Some of the farmers told us they got 70 bushels of wheat to the acre, a rather large statement, I think, but all the grain I saw was very stout, and the heads well filled, with a very plump kernel. The flour is very white and makes excellent bread, as we bought a few sacks and I had an opportunity of testing its excellence.

We had arrived nearly at the head of the Valley and were about to pass the last house when some one said, "Let us go and see what kind of folks they are," so four of us went in. The cabin was nearly square, without any floor, with a bed in the center. The mother was standing by the fireplace, and the two daughters, seventeen and nineteen, were sitting on the bed, their limbs hanging down without any shoes or stockings, and were they not dirty! Neither did the place smell but very little of roses; for civilized white folks they beat anything we had ever seen before. After asking them a few questions as regarded their prosperity, and receiving piecrust answers, we went out into the fresh air.

The seventh day from the city we came to Bear River; here at this time the ford is deep and we came very near being washed away. The forward cattle got out, then they pulled out the rest; nearly all our freight was wet, also our blankets, but the sun shone out warm and they were nearly dry by sundown. We then started on two miles when we took one more look at the great Salt Lake Valley and entered a defile of the mountains and we were in the desert again. We were obliged to travel until near midnight to find water, and that was so brackish we could not use it.

As soon as day began to break we started on again and travelled fourteen miles over a burning sand, when we came to a spring on the side of a mountain, cold and clear, and there we drank and

Chapter VIII

drank for nearly half an hour; it seemed almost impossible to quench our thirst. We could not have proceeded much further to have saved our lives. The distance travelled without water was nearly forty miles. This spring will long be remembered by those that sat around it that day. The spring is about five feet square and a foot in depth, with a gravely bottom, and one would hardly believe it could be so cold under a burning sun. Here another train was camped; they had taken what was called the "Lawson's Cut-off." This led them into an error, and a fearful desert without grass or water. They had lost so many of their cattle they were obliged to leave their wagons and were now making pack saddles to fit their oxen. They cut strips of hide from the cattle that had died, and with these they made lashings for their packs. They had three women folks and four small children; they seemed to have pretty good courage considering the bad luck they had. They said they were in hopes to get through, God willing; while there was life there was yet hope.

As we sat around our watch fires that night, and talked of dangers passed, we thought of our perilous journey yet to come, of deserts to cross, wide and deep rivers to pass over, the numerous tribes of remorseless savages to get safely by; all these changing incidents kept us far into the night. We now set the guard and the rest of us laid down to dream of our perilous way.

There being but little grass here, at daylight we went on six miles, and camped for two hours for the cattle to eat. Here we strike the alkali region. Many cattle have died here from being poisoned by drinking from alkali holes. Two days more we came to Swan Valley, and here we found grass, but poor water. Two of our cattle were taken sick by drinking alkali water, but if taken in season they can be saved by giving them two pounds of salt fat pork; this acts directly and neutralizes the poison.

The next morning one of the oxen of another train camped in the Valley and had five arrows sticking in his hide, and this being quite a large train we could muster twenty-five men, well armed, besides Jim and his frying pan. A few days before nearly a whole train of emigrants, mostly Swedes, had been destroyed by the Indians. We talked the matter over and concluded to go and wipe them

In Search of Gold

out. We sent out four men to ascertain their camp, and about nine o'clock in the forenoon our men returned and reported their camp about four miles to the North, surrounded by a thick growth of sage brush. They said they counted forty-five lodges. This was more than we had bargained for, and we held a council of war and talked the matter over; some were for charging instanter, others thought we had better let the nest alone, but the majority were for charging under cover of night and carrying the place by storm.

We now began to make preparation for the work before us. We made some torches by dipping sticks of sagebrush in our tar buckets; these were to fire the lodges as we carried the place. Five men had Colt's revolvers, besides rifles; four had breechloaders; the rest had common rifles and shotguns. I considered the shotgun much the best for a fight like that; knives we had but few; three men carried hatchets and one an axe. Thus armed, we left camp and marched silently on for nearly an hour, when we divided our men into two parties; one was to go around on the farther side of the lodges and at a signal, the bark of a coyote, both parties were to charge from all parts. We got up as near the camp as we thought it would do; as it was, two of their wolf dogs came for us; this we had expected and were prepared to meet them. These we settled with our knives without any notice. In five minutes the signal came, the yelp of a coyote, and we charged down upon the camp. The Indians came out like hornets, and we cut them down as fast as they came out, and as fast as we came in possession we fired their lodges; these being made of hides and sticks were soon destroyed. We now had the Indians between two fires, and this made them fight like demons. We charged through the camp and back, two of our boys were down, and three more were bleeding from arrow wounds, and still the savages stood up to the fight. Jim was doing fearful work with his frying pan, in fact we all had our hands full. The Indians tried to surround us, but we broke through them and charged back again. Up to that time we had not fired a gun. The order now came to retreat, that the Indians might show themselves more fully. When they saw us retreat they charged out after us, and the order now came to stand and fire. We gave them a volley at close range, and then charged

Chapter VIII

them with a yell. This was more than they could stand, and they broke and fled in all directions. We then fired all the lodges that were not consumed. The children and squaws had gone long ago, and we followed up the retreat until they were completely scattered. We now returned. Sampson and Daniels were sitting up; they had done up their cuts and one was able to march, the other we had to carry on a stretcher. Nineteen Indians laid passive and twelve showed signs of life. Jim said he must have one scalp. I said, "Take it off quick, for we must be on the move." When all was ready we started for camp, where we arrived at three o'clock in the morning. We had the four wounded men cared for the best we could under the circumstances, and camped here two days that our wounded men might recruit somewhat. We had been victorious and had given the Indians a lesson they will not forget for some time.

When we left the camp the second day, Jim tied the scalp on a stock of sagebrush, alongside of the trail, as a warning to the red men to keep civil.

From here to [along?] the Humboldt River is two hundred miles, and the land most of the way is quite broken, the soil, composed of sand and ashes; products, sage brush, sage hens and jackass rabbits. These were quite plenty and were quite acceptable after travelling all day over the burning sun. We have more or less of this for nine hundred miles, enough to dampen the courage of even the Yankees. We strike the Humboldt where it commences at a spring and travel down three hundred miles where it expands into quite a river.

The next three days were hard travelling and monotonous in the extreme. Just as we were about camping word was brought to us that Indians were coming over the hills and would soon be upon us. The order was given to unhitch the cattle and get them into the center of the camp as quick as possible; in five minutes we were ready to defend ourselves. We sent out three men to the high ground to see if the Indians were about to make an attack. The scouts returned in a few moments and said no Indians were in sight; we left one man to watch while we put up the tents and got supper. The day had been exceedingly hot and the night brought no relief.

CHAPTER IX

A Surprise — Jim and his Frying Pan — Arrive at the Humboldt — The "Diggers" — In Search of the Cattle — Attacked by a Digger — The Applegate Trail — Hard Travelling — The Boiling Spring — "Rabbit Hole Spring" — The Salt Plain — "Black Rock Boiling Springs" — Loss of Cattle — "Smoke Creek Canyon" — "Summer Valley" — The Sierra Nevada Mountains — Etc., Etc., Etc.

Indians, if they make an attack, always do so just before day, when they think their enemies are asleep. At midnight the guard was relieved and double guard was set to look out for the morning hours, when we might expect an attack. As our guard could be trusted we turned in early and soon forgot, in sleep, the troubles of life. How long I had been asleep I cannot tell, but I was suddenly awakened by my hair being pulled. I was about to spring up with a yell, but Jim said, "Be quiet and come with me." I knew something must be up, for Jim had his frying pan in his hand. He said, "Bring your double barrel gun; there is going to be some fun," and Jim liked fun as well as any man I ever saw. When we were out of the tent Jim said, "I couldn't sleep a darn wink, and I have been out beyond the

Chapter IX

guard, and if them red varmint [ain't] skulking round out there, and getting ready to come down upon us, I will eat my head." The night was quite dark and I could see nothing, I told Jim; so he said he could hear them plain enough. I laid my ear to the ground and could hear a confusion of sounds, but could not distinguish any separate one. Said I, "Jim, let us creep out carefully and ascertain what is going on." We had crawled over some twenty rods when Jim's head came in sudden contact with an Indian, and to say they two were not surprised would be telling a whopper. I knew not what had happened until Jim sprang up and brought down his frying pan with a whack on the Indian's skull that sounded like striking on an empty barrelhead. Several red skins now sprang up and I fired both barrels into them in quick succession, and then clubbed my gun and struck right and left, but the reds had fled. They had been taken by surprise themselves.

I find when thus taken their courage leaves them, and they think that is bad medicine, and away they go at the top of their speed. These belong to the Digger tribe, and they depend mostly on their numbers. My firing had brought out the guard and the whole camp, and when the statement had been made Jim was again the hero of the hour; his frying pan stood high among the implements of warfare. Dan said "You will consider this a compliment," and he picked Jim up and placed him on his shoulder and carried him to camp. Nothing more occurred that night.

In six days travel we came to the Humboldt; this stream is bordered most of the way by willows. Here the Diggers hide in the daytime and pounce upon any stragglers they find unprepared. The grass down this stream most of the way is pretty good; there seems to be a dry season here, as there has been no sign of rain for a long time; everything is parched except near the margin of the stream. Here we overtook a number of emigrants who had lost a number of their oxen; this obliged them to leave their wagons, and they were packing their cattle with their provisions. An ox looks very odd when his back is loaded in this way. How they were to cross the rivers I don't see, as part of the land would be under water; it is said where there is a will there is a way. A few had lost all their cattle and were on foot. Sink or swim, survive or perish, they must go on.

One morning while the boys (we all go by the name of boys) were yoking up the cattle I started on with my gun, (which is my constant companion) and in about a mile I met a packer coming back very much frightened. He said two Diggers had crossed the trail just above and gone into the willows, and wanted to wait until the train came up. I said, "Show me where they went in, I would try and find them," so we went on to the place where he saw them go in. I hunted high and low but could not find them.

The next night after this I and another young man had the first watch. The night being chilly we built a fire of buffalo chips; we had been talking for some time when I heard a whistle; I looked around and found the cattle gone towards the distant mountains. We both started after them on the double quick; it seemed as though they were drawn by some invisible power, for we could hardly stop them. There was a large bunch of bushes a short distance from where I stopped the cattle, and I went out towards it when up started an Indian and fired three arrows at me; one grazed my shoulder and one went through my pants; I then blazed away at him. He gave a yell and a whoop, and then ran like an antelope over the hills; we did not let the cattle get away so far again that night.

Six days travel brought us to Humboldt Meadow; the grass here is excellent. A fine meadow of some thirty acres, an oasis that is pleasant for the eye to rest upon. Here is the junction of the Applegate route, leading into Shasta, the northern part of California.

Near the source of the Sacramento River we called a council of our company to see whether we would go by the way of Carson and so come into Hangtown, the middle mines, or take the northern route to Shasta. After much discussion, it was decided to take the Applegate trail. From here it is one hundred miles without grass or water, and we now went to cutting grass and curing it for the journey. A train of seven wagons that was going by the way of Carson had a scythe; this we borrowed for one day and we considered ourselves quite fortunate, for to cut so much with knives would have been slow work. In one day we had collected all we thought we should need. We stopped here two days that the cattle might get

Chapter IX

rested for the perilous march over the desert.

The second day, early in the morning, we bid our friends of the Meadow goodbye and started on, the cattle sinking into the sand six inches, making it very hard travelling. At night we had gone over sixteen miles; here we found a very small spring from which we could give the cattle but little water, it running only a pail full in fifteen minutes. We gave the cattle some hay and took a little lunch ourselves and then started on and travelled until midnight, when we came to a boiling spring nearly hot enough to cook our coffee. The cattle were almost choked for water; we baled the water out into holes to let it cool, and in about two hours we had as much cooled off as we thought the cattle ought to drink at this time. After we got through we all turned in for a good sleep, there being no fear of Indians, as they could not exist here. When we woke up in the morning the sun was high in the heavens.

We got some breakfast and started on, and late in the afternoon we came to "Rabbit Hole Spring." This hole is about six feet deep, with green brackish water; we were so dry that we took a good drink while we held our breath, but it was horrid stuff. We cleaned the hole out and found six partly decayed rabbits in it. When sufficient water had come in we watered the cattle, gave them a foddering of hay, and as evening set in started on.

We now had forty miles to travel over a salt plain before we could get any water or grass, and for two days we had bad water to drink and we began to feel the effects of it; we wanted to hurry on that we might find something better. All through here the earth has been overturned by volcanic action; the earth is a fire red. Then come long levels, the surface smooth and hard as cement.

At sundown we started on; the night was cool and light enough to travel, and we are obliged to travel in the night on account of salt on the plain; the blistering sun shining on this injures the eyesight. Over this forty miles there is not a bush or a spear of grass, or any living thing. Here lay along the trail whole trains of oxen, wagons and chains, that had perished in 1850. The oxen lay there just as they fell; not a wolf had disturbed them in their solitary sleep; the sun had shrunk them to nearly one half their natural size, and the salt of the plain had pressured them. It was very sad to look upon all this wreck and think how much they must have suffered, and we wondered too, if there had been any loss of human life as well.

About ten the next morning we came to "Black Rock Boiling Springs;" it is nearly round and about twenty feet across; the water is nearly boiling hot, and it only requires a few moments fire to have it boil. It runs down one hundred yards into holes to receive it, where it is cooled off for the use of the cattle. These springs remind one of the hot place down below where the fire is unquenchable.

A party of the boys went out on a voyage of discovery and in an hour came in and reported grass two miles to the east, and the cattle were then driven up and a party went to cut hay for the next two days travel.

The next day at four in the afternoon we started for "Deep Water Wells," forty-three miles distant. The day before we had lost a number of our cattle and were obliged to throw away everything that was not actually needed; one ox we had left yesterday came up just as we were starting on again; he lay down and we went up and patted him and he tried to get up to go with us, but he had got to the end of his journey and we left him there with the solitude.

The trail during the night was hard and nearly water level, the crust of salt making it equal to moonlight. At sunrise we came to a small knoll of sand where we got some breakfast, fed the cattle, and then went down (we name the place Hades) to a place a little below the level of the plain. There was a cauldron some thirty feet across and some eight feet in the center, and the water was boiling up over four feet; it sounded like distant thunder; one would say the fires were not very distant, but the boiling seemed to be somewhat fitful as it would boil higher at times and then go down a little. It seems the trade winds blow here for the border around this cauldron is very green, except on the west side, and there it is kept bare by the steam that arises like a cloud. Some ten rods to the east there was a hole where the fire had sometime been at work; we could look down, down into the undisturbed depth below.

After stopping two hours we proceeded on to the "Wells," which was thirteen miles. The sand being deep we travelled slow, and the

Chapter IX

day was very warm too. We thought at one time the cattle could not reach it, but after a good deal of urging we arrived about dark. This was an oasis such as we had not seen for many a day. It contained some four acres of nice grass and a little lake of water some thirty feet wide and sixty feet long and over eighty feet deep, according to bubble measure, cold and very clear, but not a fish or a living thing in it. We stopped here two days to recruit the cattle. This few acres of land was surrounded by a desert of forty miles. All this vast solitude must once have been a part of the Pacific Ocean.

The third day, early in the morning, we started for "Smoke Creek Canyon," fifty-three miles distant, and this was the hardest tramp on the whole route. We arrived at the Canyon about midnight. All this distance the sand and ashes is some six inches deep and the ashes made a tremendous dust that clogged the lungs badly; how those cattle did cough! The day was exceedingly warm, the sun shining with that brilliancy that is only seen on a sandy desert, and the blistering heat seemed to dry up the little blood left in our veins. Jim said our business, as it looks, was over, as everything we had seen dried and shrivelled; in fact our provisions were running short.

The night was very dark and we could proceed no further that night. We were very tired and hungry and so were the poor cattle upon which we depended so much; we all laid down where we stood without unhitching. As soon as light the next morning we started on six miles, when we came to a beautiful meadow with a clear stream of water running through the center, and here we camped Saturday and Sunday. This little valley contains some fifty or more acres and would make a nice farm; the grass was excellent and it stood about three feet high and of good quality; the murmuring brooklet as its clear water dashed over the crystallized rocks, was indeed a pleasant sight for the eye to rest upon, after passing that terrible waste that has burned into my mind to last to the end of my existence.

After breakfast the boys went out with their guns on the mountains and were gone until noon, but saw nothing that had life—on the top of the highest mountain they found crystallized rock, some specimens of which were very pretty, shaped like diamonds and

In Search of Gold

clear as water. I think there must be gold here from the indication, and if I had tools I should have prospected. We had thrown them away on account of the cattle giving out.

Monday morning we rolled out for "Summer Valley," eighteen miles distant. The first mile up the valley and our little brooklet had sunk; in half a mile it again came to the surface. I should have liked to penetrate that cavern, lit up with tons of burnished gold and listened to the tramp of the invisible.

CHAPTER X

Hunting for Provisions — The Grizzly Bear — The Indian Devil — Deer and Antelope — Lose Another Wagon and Oxen — A Forest on Fire — "Pine Meadow" — "Pleasant Valley" — "Mount Shasta" — Short of Provisions — Kill a Buck — Meet with Indians — Lost in the Forest — Attacked by Indians — Hunting for the Trail — Etc., Etc., Etc.

The next day a number of us went out to hunt our provisions were nearly exhausted and starvation began to look as though it meant business. Dan brought in one deer, quite a good-sized buck; this was the first live object we had seen for three hundred miles. We were now obliged to stand guard nights for we had seen signs of Indians around, and that, too, in large numbers. The nights, as we ascend, are growing quite cool and a fire in the evening to sit by is quite comfortable, and we could bear an extra blanket if we had one.

The next day we saw the first bear track and fourteen of us, well armed, started in pursuit. Mr. Grizzly had gone along the trail that night, for they are nightwalkers as well as some others. He kept

In Search of Gold

along the trail some six miles when the track led off into some bushes; a short distance and we came to where an ox had died, only the bones were left; the paths made by the bears around the carcass indicated that they were very numerous. We went on a short distance and came to a place that had been burnt over, and as we came to the top of the hill I looked down and saw the ashes fly around the end of a big log. Said I, "Boys, there he goes," and we all took after him as fast as the nature of the ground would permit, until we came to some bushes. We heard a cracking in there that made us stop and hesitate what we had better do. When we had penetrated a few feet one man sang out, "There are two of them;" another man said, "Don't a man fire, if you do we are gone up." We now walked out of that, and not as though we were going to a day's work either; there were paths all through the bushes showing them to be as thick as three in a bed. Wishing to hunt, but not be hunted, we went back to the trail, but before we got there we saw a gun standing up against a tree; it must have been left there the season before from the condition it was in. The man must have been treed by a grizzly and chewed up when he came down.

We found a spring just before night where we camped among the giant trees that had to all appearances stood there for centuries; if a bear should make his appearance we could find none small enough to climb.

The next day we travelled twenty-five miles and came to a spring about ten in the evening. We killed two deers today, which was just in season to keep our courage up. Just before camping we saw a California lion pass down the hollow and cross the trail not thirty rods from camp.

We are now obliged to build a large fire every night to keep the wild animals from attacking us; the dismal howl of the grey wolf can be heard every night, as well as other sounds, showing this vast forest is thickly settled. Last night we heard an Indian devil cry out like a female in distress. Jim answered the cry and we found the creature as he answered was coming nearer; all hands got ready with their guns and Jim held his frying pan behind him as he answered. This animal springs from tree to tree; and if within reach, they thus have

Chapter X

the advantage of lighting on their prey unawares, and having long hook-nails they tear out whatever they take hold of. We now took up positions, each one behind a tree, and awaited the result. He seemed to be coming quite slow and at one time we thought he had given up and slid to the ground. Jim gave a very weak cry and the next instant we saw him, by the light of the campfire, spring from a tree into another within range; six of us were now ordered to fire and the others to be ready in case we failed to bring him down. The six were nearly as one report; he made a spring for another tree but missed it and came to the ground. How he made the dirt and leaves fly for a few moments! It was the most vicious creature I had ever seen. Old Burr knew enough to keep out of his way, and Jim gave him a whack with his frying pan that ended his career.

The next day we came to "Hunting Valley" and here we saw thousands of deer and antelope; not much hunting to do here. In less than two hours we brought in seven deer and two antelope, the first we had killed on the mountain. The antelope is considered by the hunters the nicest meat that runs, and I can say it was good enough when one has a forest appetite, as I had. The trail here is very crooked, winding among these immense trees that seem to have no end.

The next morning we left another wagon with all its fixtures; four more of our oxen were unable to move on and we left them there for the grizzly bears. In twelve miles we came to the mountain ridge. This is the largest opening we had seen since ascending the mountain. Half a mile from camp we found a splendid valley containing about one hundred acres, covered with a heavy growth of grass. As we were driving the cattle down there we saw a novel sight; this was a long line of white pelicans feeding; that was what we called them from the description given in books. The boys tried to get a shot at them, but they had wings as well as legs and away they went to some unknown pond or lake, where the sound of the rifle has not been heard. Our camp was on the highest point of the mountain this night, and it was very cold, so cold we could not sleep. We built several large fires to keep from freezing and keep the wild animals away. It makes one's hair stand on end to hear them scream, roar and yell like fiends incarnate. The roar of the grizzly bear could be heard above all the rest having a tussle, perhaps with a pointer, or panther.

The next morning we started on the descent and travelled slow; the forest had taken fire, or been set by the red men, and was burning furiously. This was slow and dangerous work; in many places burning trees and limbs lay across the trail, and a detachment went on ahead with axes to clear the way. In many places we had to make a detour of some distance before we could again take the trail. We called this the passage of Hades; brands of fire dropped upon the cattle, the wagon covers took fire several times, also our clothes, but the hardest part was for the cattle's feet, for we were forced to run them through places of burning coals and hot ashes; how it did burn them!

After passing through this fiery ordeal, in five miles we came to "Pine Meadow," where we found a nice spring and plenty of grass. We thought it best to camp over one day to let the cattle rest, for we were fearful they would give out. Before we got through here we saw plenty of bear tracks, they stay largely where they can obtain water handily.

From here to "Pleasant Valley" is two days' travel over a black sand that we sink into very deep. This is the hardest travelling we have found in crossing the mountain; ten miles a day was all we could make. We are now in the earthquake region; in crossing a hollow we heard some heavy body become detached from under us as we passed over, and it seemed two or three minutes before we heard the report of its fall, which seemed to be a very heavy body. There must have been a tremendous vacuum down there. Not more than a mile from there we came to a mountain of cinders and several of us tried to ascend to the crater; this was hard work as the cinders gave way beneath our feet, cutting our boots badly. Jim was the only one that succeeded in attaining the top and he looked very small up so high. He said the crater was not more than six feet across, but slanting down to it for some way in the distance, he said he could see Shasta Buke [Butte] or Mount Shasta as some call it. A little farther on there has been an earthquake of recent date; large trees have been overthrown, ashes and cinders cover the earth. We now wind in and out among the debris and a little further on we come to a

Chapter X

small lake formed by the upheaval. The water is of a clear green color and it is very deep, and yet bottom can be seen as well as the top. This is quite remarkable; not a fish or a living thing near it.

We are now among the eternal sandbar. Here we see it black as night that has been there for centuries; some five or six miles have been thrown into every shape conceivable, some of the highest points covered with recent snow falls. It was a most desolate and lonesome region and the place reminded me of the *Miner's Lament,* a short poem I saw in a paper printed in Stockton, called the *Surface Diggins,* printed in 1850, the first two verses I remember quite well:

High on a rough and dismal crag
Where kern light spout, aye there's the rub
Where oft no doubt some midnight hag
Had danced a jig with Beelzebub.

Then wake ye storms, my wild tin pan,
Afright the crickets from their lairs,
Make wood and mountain ring again,
And terrify the grizzly bears.

We hurried over through this place as fast as possible and in ten miles came to a place that was covered with a heavy growth of wood. Some forty rods from the trail we found a nice spring of water where we made our camp for the night; we were getting down where it is much warmer. This day we saw large numbers of deer and we saw two large animals cross the trail. None of us knew what they were; they seemed to be in pursuit of something. While eating supper old Burr came limping in badly torn by some wild beast he had come in contact with on his raids after deer. We tied up the wounds the best we could, but he whined bitterly most of the night. He had been a faithful friend on the Plains through the long watches of the night.

Early the next morning we rolled on; our flour and bacon all gone, and we had rather a light breakfast of venison; so all those that could be spared from driving went out each side of the trail to hunt. I did not intend to go far, but when in pursuit of game one passes over more ground without knowing it than he would if he had been hoeing corn. I had not gone more than half a mile when a short distance ahead lay a large tree that had fallen, and just over the top I could see the antlers of a buck and the hind quarters of another one at the end of the log. I fired at that one and knocked him over; three more started out into sight and I gave one a charge of buckshot and then all three ran off. I loaded again and after hanging the one killed up on a tree the best I could, I started on after the others; they did not go far before they stopped to see what it was after them. I got up within twenty rods and then fired, one dropped and then got up and ran after the others.

I stopped and charged the rifle barrel and went on, for I was quite sure I had given one the death blow, and so it proved; in going some sixty rods I came to a hollow and there were three Indians skinning my deer. I got up as near as I could, and not be seen; they were busy tearing out the entrails, and before they had finished taking off the skin I thought they had gone far enough and I gave a yell; they jumped up, I presented my gun, they threw up their hands and took to their heels. Most of the people crossing the plains think them fair game, but I could not think so, and so let them go. If they had attacked me the case would have been different.

I hung this carcass on a tree. I had heard no guns as I expected I should from some of the others that had gone out, and I thought it best to find the trail and so took the bearing as I thought that way and walked pretty fast. To be lost in a great forest like that was not very pleasant to think of. I had travelled nearly an hour and still no trail did I come to. I then said, well, I am in for it and no mistake. I then turned half around and started off as though I had been called to dinner. I walked for half an hour and travelled over a long distance, coming within range of both deer and antelope, but I cared not for them or those I had slain.

The forest was so still one could have heard a pin drop if there had been one; this had a depressing influence over my thoughts and I said, "Confound the luck, I shall have to build me a shanty, and

Chapter X

there will be another Robinson Crusoe;" as I said this I stepped behind a large tree as I had spied a half dozen red skins and I thought it would be an easy matter to obtain a man Friday. I stayed under cover until they had passed out of sight. I now took off my vest and put it on wrong side out, as I had heard that everything would come around right again if this was done, but all to no purpose. The sun remained just where it seemed it ought not to, then I looked for moss that usually grows on the north side of trees, but I found it all the same; then I thought of the breeze that was blowing in the morning when I started out, but it came in my face as I crossed the trail, but now there was not a breath of air stirring, the tree tops arising up out of sight.

I then looked for a tree that I could climb, this was a difficult thing to do, as most of them ran up a hundred feet without even a knot hole, but at last I found one that stood quite near another, an oak, and by placing a large limb against one I managed to get up, but what a dizzy height. I went up what I thought was two hundred feet and then looked up, and found it was a long distance still; I was rising in the world, that was something, and so I continued to climb, and at last reached the topmost limb. What a disappointment, there were other trees higher and I could see nothing; one thing I felt, the breeze, and noted the direction from whence it came. I now commenced my descent and by good luck landed on the ground once more and started off with new courage.

I hadn't gone more than a mile when I came in sight of five Digger Indians; they saw me at the same time and I must face the music; they were not long in observing there was but one and they made up their minds to have my scalp. That I could see at once, as they sent a flight of arrows directly my way, but expecting something of that kind, I jumped behind a tree, when they made a dash for my position. Before they could come upon me, I stepped out and brought down two of them; they were close together and I had a good shot. Two more had received shot from the way they howled and jumped about; three of them now got behind trees.

I loaded as quick as possible and as I was ramming down the last cartridge I heard footsteps near by; I looked up and if there wasn't

Dan Vernotten not two yards away. I sang out, "Look out, Dan, there are Indians here!" The Indians were now skulking from tree to tree and both of us took after them; as one came out from behind a tree Dan fired but missed; I was near enough and gave him some more buckshot before he got to cover behind a tree. Dan had again loaded and was going after them, but I said, "They will not trouble us any more; let us find the trail;" he looked around and then pointed to the two reds on the ground and said, "I heard those two shots and felt a great relief for I have been lost ever since morning. I have killed four deer and have seen lots more." He said he had not seen an Indian all day. I don't think the world ever knew two men that were more glad to see each other than ourselves.

The next thing was to find the trail, and we started in the direction I had taken when I met the reds. We had travelled more than two hours, for the sun was getting quite low, when we came to a place where the large trees were quite scattering and the undergrowth was very thick, consisting of a kind of dwarf oak from four to six feet in height loaded with acorns. All among these bushes were hard beaten paths and we saw by the tracks that they were made by bears after acorns. Dan says, "Now look out for bears." "You are right," said I; "hark, I think I hear one now." We both listened and could hear one pulling down the bushes to get the nuts. Says Dan, "I am going to have that grizzly." I said, "Don't disturb them kind of folks; they are not friendly, and besides we must find the trail." "Darn the trail; I am going for that bear," and away he strode among the bushes. I followed and it was not more than three minutes before he fired and was coming my way on the full jump, with a big grizzly in close pursuit. I stepped out one side and as he came by I poured in my two charges, but more than twenty feet away; the rifle ball broke his shoulder, still he did not halt, but could not get on so fast, and Dan soon loaded again. He had taken after me, so I could not load and ran and I was obliged to do the latter until Dan came up and fired again, the ball passing through the brain. This closed the contest although we left him kicking. "Well," I said, "Dan, are you willing to look for the trail now?" "Yes," he said, "now we have killed the bear."

CHAPTER XI

Meet with Indians — Bear River — The Indian and His Squaw — Arrival at "Fort Redding" — Tired and Hungry — The Cook and the Friendly Irishman — Leave the Fort — Arrival of the Train — Jim's Story — The Auction — Commence Mining — Bear and Bull Fight — Etc., Etc., Etc.

In twenty minutes we came to the trail, about a dozen bears had gone along from the looks of their footprints, but our train had not yet come up. It was getting towards night and it was some twenty five miles to Redding's Fort [Fort Reading], on Cow Creek. We had gone along the trail about two miles, when looking over on the left of the trail where it was quite open, we saw some twenty-five Indians dressed in war paint. They were about forty rods from the trail, and they seemed to be holding a council around a large sugar pine. Dan espied them the same time that I did, and he up with his rifle and would have fired if I had not pulled his gun down; still he wanted to bring down an Injun, as he said. When he raised his rifle every bow was raised, and I told Dan if he fired he would kill but one and there would be twenty four left to take our scalps. I said the odds were too great, and besides they have made no attack upon us, so I prevailed on him to come on the double quick.

At sundown we came to Bear River; we were very tired and hungry, having eaten nothing since morning. The stream was cold and clear, and we thought we would bathe, for it would be refreshing and take some of the tired from our limbs. We set our guns up against a tree near by, that in case of danger we could take them on in an instant.

We had sat down to take our boots off and when looking up I saw a dust rise on the other bank. Said I, "Dan, take your rifle; there is something coming over on the other bank." We stood waiting for what might turn up, and pretty soon two heads popped up; we raised our guns to fire when they threw their hands up, as much as to say "Don't." They proved to be only an Indian and his squaw; she had a large basket of grapes on her head. The man came across and then told his squaw to come, and when she had crossed he took the basket off her head and took out a double handful of grapes and offered them to Dan. As Dan did not offer to take them I held out my hat and he filled it full; he seemed very much pleased to see how handy a hat was; perhaps he may have one some time, as he had none on, or anything else. He sat there some time trying to tell us something. We could not make out what it was, and they soon went away, but we concluded not to bathe at this time.

We are now at the foothills, on the Pacific slope; the Plains and the Nevadas have been passed, and still we keep our scalps. We had left that boundless forest full of wild men and animals; we had left our comrades there too, how far back we knew not; they had camped long ago, and no doubt had given us up as lost. The day had been very warm, and we had left our coats in the wagon in the morning, but now we wanted them much, as the nights become quite cool.

We now hurried on as fast as we could; we saw by the tracks that two bears had gone on ahead of us. Dan said, "Perhaps they have gone on to the fort to enlist as heavy dragoons." Their tracks continued along the trail as long as we could see.

We were now well out of trees of any kind, and appeared to be

Chapter XI

travelling over a level plain, and we expected every moment that we should come in contact with some of those night walkers that are somewhat tough in their embrace. Every little while we stopped and listened, that we might not be taken by surprise.

We continued to travel until we heard the joyful sound of an axe; some one was splitting up kindlings for morning; this gave us new courage and we walked on.

In a short time we came to Cow Creek; this was quite a deep stream and we were obliged to take our clothes off and wade; this was cold work as the water was from melting snows in the mountains. As soon as we had passed we received a challenge: "Who goes there?" I said, "Friends." "Then give the countersign." I said, "Is this the fort?" He said "Yes, this is Fort Redding." "Well," said I, "I have no countersign except that we have just crossed over the mountains and are very hungry." I asked what he was doing there and he said guarding government stock, mules and oxen. I asked if there would be any show for us to get anything to eat. He pointed to a distant light and said, "That light comes from the cook room; the cook is a good fellow and will give you something." He could not see how we had travelled so far in the night without having been destroyed by the reds or bears. He said, "A man was killed at the Fort last evening; one came on the parade ground and a dozen soldiers fired at him; he crawled in under some chaparral and a soldier crawled in after him, armed with a Colt's revolver; he came upon the bear before he was aware of his presence, and the bear struck him down with his paw, taking one side of his face off clean; a whole detachment of soldiers were now called out and they all poured in a volley, and Bruin rolled over. The wounded man was taken to the Fort, but died in a few moments." This was the sentry's story. We now bid the sentry good night and went for the light we had spotted some time before.

In a short distance we came to another stream; this was Little Cow Creek, not so deep as the other, but with a swift current over loose cobble stones. We were surprised to find the Fort had no wall, ditch, or drawbridge, and so we went up to the cook room unmolested. As we went in the clock indicated half past eleven. The cook said, "Well, boys, what is up now?" I said, "There is nothing up, except we are very hungry, and we have made you a friendly call, hoping you would give us something to keep our insides from coming together." He said it was late and against orders, but he thought none of the officers would be apt to come in now, it being so late; so he went to work and gave a good nice supper, a good big slice of the late grizzly making it substantial. I asked him if there was any show for us under cover to sleep. He said we had better go to the officers' quarters, and they would give us a permit; so we went out and into a building that was somewhat better than the others. Two men were smoking at the far end, with a gold band around their caps; one of them spoke up and said, "What do you want in here?" I waited for Dan to speak, but he said nothing. The officer again asked what we wanted, in a very loud tone, thinking to scare somebody. I said, "Gentlemen, we are emigrants from over the mountain; we are ahead of our train, and having left our coats with the wagons and the night under cover." He said, "Our men lay down on the ground anywhere, so can you," and then went to talking with his companion. I said, "Can't you lend us a blanket?" "No, they had none." We bid them good evening and went out around to the parade ground; there we found a sentry with a good fire to keep him warm and keep off the bears that are always prowling around in the night time. The sentry was an Irishman, and when he saw our condition, he said, "You stay here while I go and investigate." Pretty soon he returned and said, "There are some tents under yonder shed; go and get two of them and spread them down here by the fire. It was quite comfortable to sleep by a fire, with a sentinel to keep off the bears. He made us promise to take the tents back in the morning before the morning officer made his rounds. This we thought would be easy enough, considering how late they sat up. The sentry said he was breaking orders, but orders or no orders, we should be protected from the weather. At two o'clock the sentry was changed, but our Irishman said he would stand guard until morning as he could not trust the other one; this was proving him to be a friend indeed. Just before day he shook us up and said, "Get up quick and take those tents back. I have let you sleep up to the last minute."

Chapter XI

We were up in less than no time, and carried the tents back where we found them. "Now," he says, "You stay around here and I will see that you have some breakfast." So we waited until near seven, when we received an invitation to come and get our rations, which we did; it consisted of coffee, hard bread, and a piece of corned beef; this was our first and last meal of victuals obtained from Uncle Sam. We now found our friendly Irishman and thanked him heartily for his disinterested kindness to us. We shook him by the hand and started on up the valley.

This station stands on a high plateau between the Sacramento River and Cow Creek and they tell me that it is difficult to enlist men to keep up their campment, for the Indians slide in and take a good many scalps. There is nothing that an Indian delights in so much as a soldier's scalp.

We went up the valley six miles and obtained board until our train should come up. Sacramento River at this point is not very wide, not over forty yards, and quite shallow, with many falls, and we could see many salmon jumping out of the water.

The next day, towards night, our train came up. Jim gave me a regular bear hug. He said he had not slept a wink since I had been gone. I told him of being lost in the forest, our Indian and bear fight, and our experience at the fort. "Well," he said, "You are very lucky to have kept your scalp, and I am glad you did. Now let me tell you our troubles since you left. We travelled until noon, as usual, and turned out for the cattle to rest and get a bite of something to eat. We had eaten our dinner when about twenty Indians charged into our camp. You know that you were always looking for Indians, and so was always ready for them; but we took but little thought about them, and now we were not ready to give them that reception they should have had. I clinched my frying pan and first gave them the hot fat that was in it. I then gave them the outside with all my might, my soul and strength; they went right through the camp and knocked over everything; only five of the guns were loaded and these did good service. Thomas distinguished himself in a masterly manner; that little crowbar we had, you know, that we were going to throw away at Pleasant Valley; well Tom got hold of that, and

In Search of Gold

how those Indians went down under his blows. In five minutes the reds had gone, that is, what were able to go. Nine lay stretched out on the ground, food for the grey wolf; but as you see, Simon is not here; we buried him nearly a mile this side of the battlefield that the reds may not take off his scalp, he fought well, poor fellow, but he stood in the way of an arrow that penetrated his breast. Larn was wounded in his leg, but not bad and there is a mark I received from an arrow when I threw the hot fat. Besides the woods took fire when they charged into the camp, knocking the fire brands in all directions. As soon as the fight was over we all turned to and put it out, for we did not care to travel through another gauntlet of fire. In the afternoon we found our deer hung up alongside the trail. It was one that Dan had killed, I thought; well, when it came night and you and Dan failed to come in, we felt quite sure the reds or grizzly had got you. We talked of nothing else until we turned in; what a place that was for bears! I am very sure I saw five; none of us dared to molest them. This morning we started early and here we are; by the way, a few miles the other side of the fort, we saw your tracks along the trail. We knew one was you, because you toe out so much more than any of the rest." I said, "I see one ox less here." "Yes," he said, "we left old red; he could not get up this morning; he was not to see the promised land; and also poor Simon, so near and yet not to see that land of gold he had travelled so far to behold."

This was Jim's story. How much we may be thankful for that we came through safe that afternoon!

Some of the boys went around to notify those wishing to purchase what things there was left, three yoke of oxen and one wagon out of eighteen yoke of oxen and six wagons that we started with.

At ten o'clock the next morning the auction began. Baptista, one of our men, was salesman. The oxen brought $120 the yoke; the average cost in Illinois was $52; the wagon brought $80.

At noon, after getting some dinner, we took our packs on our backs and started for Shasta, sixteen miles distant, where we arrived about sundown and put up at a shanty called the "American Hotel." Here we stayed until the next day, when Burton let himself as hostler for $75 a month. Jim and the Frenchman went down to Red-

Chapter XI

ding's Fort and found a place there at $50 a month.

After stopping in Shasta two days we concluded to buy a few tools and some provisions, such as flour and bacon, and start for Churn Creek, eight miles distant. There being eight of us, we formed ourselves into two companies. In four miles we came to the Sacramento River; here is a ferry, and the man charged us a dollar each to take us across. A mile this side of the creek there had been quite a village, but now all but two of the cabins were deserted; one of those we took possession of and made ourselves quite comfortable.

The next morning we went down to the Creek to prospect for those sparkling particles that have made so much trouble in the world. The Creek was entirely dried up, except now and then a small hole, and we took our dirt to these holes to wash. I was the only one that had ever dug gold, and from the prospects we got I thought we could do no better, so we took possession of enough ground to last all winter. We concluded it would be better to build our cabin down to the Creek, that we might be near our work. Our friends occupying the two cabins said it would be dangerous to live down there alone on account of the Pine River Indians. They said they had killed several miners last winter, but we concluded to build nevertheless. Four of the boys went up to Shasta and bought four Colt's navy size revolvers, and with these they went into practice that they might become proficient in their use.

We now chose a sight for our cabin and began to fell timber to build with, thirty feet long and fourteen feet wide, with a fireplace at each end, the door in the middle. There were trees enough close by to build it; to cover it was the most difficult part, but we found a large pine that would split very well; the logs were cut into four feet lengths and then quartered, and then with an implement called a frow, with this strips six and eight inches wide very much like clapboards, and put on about the same way; this makes a roof that turns the water very well. Then the chimney is built on the outside, with sticks and mud, and plastered on the inside with the same; this answers very well until it takes fire, which is quite often. We being all ready we had nothing to do but wait for the rainy season to commence; for a few days we went prospecting for some distance but

In Search of Gold

found nothing better. One day there was to be a bear and bull fight up at Shasta; six of us went up and paid two dollars a ticket to see the performance. The enclosure was a circle twelve feet high, with seats two-thirds the way round. The performance opened at one o'clock sharp; the bear was a grizzly, weight about eight hundred pounds; the bull was a Spanish black, weight twelve hundred; the bull was fastened by the fore leg, the bear by the hind leg, the chains were fastened so that they would cross without entangling. A Mexican rode into the enclosure on horseback to see that everything was all right, then he rode out; the gate was shut and then the door was raised in the cage that held the bear; grizzly did not take the hint to come out directly, until the bull came round into sight, then he dashed out; the bull went for him very quick. Bruin did not care to fight and so ran away, the bull came up and gave him a punch, then the bear turned and got between the bull's horns and I thought he would tear them out by the roots, but they were too firmly fixed. All this time the bear kept up a continual roar that could be heard two miles away; the bull soon shook him off and then gave him an Irish hoist; the bear would then turn and with his paw scrape down his side, taking the hair and in some places the hide as well. Once the bull caught him on his horn and gave him quite a toss; this made the bear mad and he came back and got hold of his hind leg, girdling it pretty badly, the bull keeping very quiet the while. The day was very warm and both animals became very hot; cold water was thrown on them but done little good. The bear would look up at the audience from time to time, as much as to say, "Who are the biggest brutes to set us here at each other?" At last the bear got a good lick at the bull and knocked him down; the bull did not offer to get up, and the bear sitting on his haunches with his tongue out, nearly blowed. After a while he thought he would see if the bull was dead or playing possum; he gave him a bite on the middle of the back. I never saw an animal come to his feet so quick as that bull did, and at it they went again, but soon gave it up, they were so hot. As the bear came round the cover to his cage was raised and in he went, the bull was so badly torn they took him out and turned him into beef. The next day another bull took his place, and the second pass

Chapter XI

he caught the bear under the throat, the horn penetrated the flesh, cutting his throat as well as could be done with a knife, he bleeding to death in a few moments.

CHAPTER XII

Voting for President — Free Run — In the Mines — The Rainy Season — Out of Flour — Dan and the Mule — Frightening the Indians — Parting with Old Companions — Meet with a Friend — In the Mud — Red Bluff — Arrive at Sacramento — Start for Weaver's Creek — Stockton — Out of Money and Provisions — Etc., Etc., Etc.

November had come and the election of President Pierce was on the tapis. We were notified to come to the polls at a mining camp called "Hard Scrabble;" "String Town" was also hard by; so in the evening the whole camp at Churn Creek, about twenty, went up. They had only one man to vote for, and that was Pierce, free rum, and a plenty of it. They all took a drink except Thomas and I; then we all went up and put in our vote; in about ten minutes another drink and go up and vote; then another ten minutes and up and vote. Seeing there was two of us that did not drink the others said we must drink too, if we did not force would be used. We said it gave us the nose bleed, and they said we should have it if we did not drink; but we were determined not to drink if it were possible. We both stood together and a good deal of bad rum was split before they

Chapter XII

succeeded. They all went up, drank and voted, until they had drank and voted ten times; they called that fun and having a good time and exercising the right of suffrage. I should say it was giving that right a big airing. After a time their heads getting light they seemed anything but what they should have been; at last they were prevailed upon to return to camp.

About breakfast time the next day we went up to a sawmill, some four miles, and bought boards for a tom and sluice to mine with; that was quite a little exercise to lug green boards four miles, but the most of them needed a sweat and it done them good. This sawmill cut six boards at a time, six saws being together; the power was a fifteen feet bucket wheel, with a high pressure of water.

The 8th of November the rainy season set in, and we all went to work, some with cradles and some with sluices. We worked a week and averaged about two dollars each; this barely furnished grub, and making long days too; it wasn't very pleasant, either, as it rained most of the time. We had several light snow falls the following week, the ground being frozen in places quite hard. One other company near by was doing quite well and they wanted us to join them, so we did and worked several days; three of us took out fifty dollars a day; this was to be divided among so many that each man's share was small. The creek now being full of water we could do but little there, and as the other company had some pay dirt thrown up in piles in the smaller runs, and as this had to be washed while it was raining, I took my rocker and worked at this for some time, washing out about six dollars a day. One day we were out of flour, and I started for Shasta and bought fifty pounds and brought it back on my shoulder, it raining hard all day. In coming down the mountain on the right bank of the river, it being very steep and the ground being slippery, I slipped and then slid about ten rods, stripping my clothes half off and getting some bad scratches; this was a locomotion I had not bargained for, and it was a wonder that I did not go into the river. I did not arrive at camp until late in the evening, entirely tired out; the boys were waiting for my arrival with hungry expressions, having had nothing to eat of bread kind all day. I then had to go to work and make some bread before we had any supper, and it seemed as if those men would eat until morning. I never fairly understood what the women folks had to do until I had made up seven or eight barrels of flour into bread. I don't think they are given but little credit for what they do.

Dan had bought a mule, for what purpose I don't think he knew himself; it cost him eighty dollars, and he thought he would take a ride one day, having bought a bridle and a Spanish saddle. It took four of us to put them and Dan on, but we succeeded at last, the mule went off like a shot down the gulch; Dan's hat came off but he hung on, and just as he was going to cross over the mule stopped so sudden that Dan went right over the mule's head into the water. We all ran down to see if he was hurt, but we found him all right except a good soaking; the water had saved his bones. We asked Dan if we should help him on again, and he said "No, not if I know myself. I don't ride that earthquake again."

I went out with a gun and had very good luck, bringing in two dozen quails; these birds are very plenty through here, and we see large flocks of them every day.

The next day, Sunday, two Pine River Indians came in to camp in order to spy around, and we sent them off on the double quick. When they had got some forty odd rods away, three of the boys tried their revolvers on them, firing as fast as they could; how those reds did run! This was so they might report the condition we were in to receive them if they should think best to try it on.

We were not making anything and Dan said he should start out and try for something better. I said "I am with you," and so the next morning early we shook hands with our companions that had been with us so long, and had been through so many trials hand in hand and shoulder to shoulder, having travelled six months in a common brotherhood, and passed over three thousand miles in perfect harmony. There are but few companies that have passed over these Plains that have agreed so well and have been so fortunate as to see the promised land without losing more from among them. My two blankets I gave away as I had a nice buffalo robe that I bought of a Crow Indian on the Plains for three dollars. This was quite heavy to carry, and not knowing how long we might have to tramp it, and

Chapter XII

Dan having two good blankets, I thought this would do. We took our guns and the mule, intending to dispose of them at the first opportunity.

We now walked on and arrived at Shasta in the afternoon, and before night Dan had sold the mule for the same as it cost him, also his gun and old Burr. Burr had to be fastened up until we had started off.

The next morning we went around among the mines but could find nothing that suited us. I had not disposed of my gun, and this was all the capital I had. One man at the hotel where we stayed said I could sell it at the Fort; he knew a man there that wanted one; so the next morning Dan and I started for the Fort, as we intended to go to Sacramento City, five hundred and forty miles distant. Rivers, creeks, gulches, and all streams at this time were carrying their full capacity of water, and some had a large surplus, and it was all returning again from whence it came. This proved a wet walk for those eighteen miles, and in some places we had to take off our pants; no bridges or planks to help one over.

We arrived at the Fort about dark and Jim was glad to see us. He asked more than fifty questions before I could answer one, and he finally calmed down and began to talk rational. He said he heard we were digging out gold by the ton and would soon start for home, and he said he was coming up to see us before we started, but a man there could not go out anywhere without a permit. He said he liked the place; there was not much work to do and a plenty to eat. Said I, "Jim, I should like to see you swing that frying pan once more, but I suppose it is entirely out of your line of business now." He said, "Yes, I am driving a four horse mule team, and I am swinging a whip; that is most of the work." I said, "They tell me up at Shasta that this Fort is a useless cost to Uncle Sam, as they cannot get the men to go after the Indians when they are called for." "Yes, that is talked over by the privates, and why they are not sent out they cannot tell; the Indians are committing more or less murders all the time." Jim felt sorry we had done no better, and he said there was a chance here ten days ago, but they were full now. Jim found a man that bought my gun, but I could get only eight dollars for it. How I hated to give it up, for we had been close companions for a long time, and it had saved my life many times too. We talked until late into the night before we retired to rest. The next morning we bid Jim goodbye and wished him success wherever he went, and he, yes, he wished us well, and more, he hoped to meet us in the life beyond; tears were running down Jim's checks as we marched away, and I have never seen him since.

We travelled all that day but could find nothing to do, and at night we slept under some brush, wet, cold and hungry. The morning we started on and in two miles came to a little log cabin where lived an old black man and his woman. We asked for some breakfast and offered to pay for it, but he said he was all out of bread and had nothing but a few potatoes; he said they were very poor and so we thought ourselves.

We now went on, and about noon we came to where a man was camped for noon, with his team loaded with provisions for the mines. He was cooking bacon, which had a pleasant smell to us, and we said we should like to join him in such pleasant work. We told him our condition, and he cut off several more rashers of bacon, and with a pot of hot coffee we made a good meal for which we offered him pay, but he would not accept anything. We thanked him kindly and started on for we wanted to reach Red Bluffs before night.

What a land this is; in the rainy season all mud and soft clay. We met several teams loaded for the mines, some were stuck beyond relief, except to unload. At one place they were drawing through a gully; thirteen yoke of oxen were hitched to a wagon whose wheels were entirely submerged, and it seemed to slide through rather than roll, and those teamsters were up to their hips in mud! Well we had been through some bad places, but nothing so dirty as that.

A little before night we arrived at Red Bluff, the head of navigation of the Sacramento River. Here we got some supper and a chance on the floor to spread our blankets; they charged here one dollar and a half a meal. A small wharf had been built here for the use of small vessels. A small steamboat was going to leave there in the morning for Sacramento City, five hundred miles away, so we engaged our passage to that city thinking we could do better than

Chapter XII

anywhere else. After paying my passage I had one and a half dollars left, and on this I must live until our arrival at the city. The current being swift and a good head of steam on, we went very fast; there were only four men to run the boat, two at night and two in the day. We came on board without any provisions, and they would not sell us any, so we had to wait until they stopped to wood up, which they did not until the next morning. About eight o'clock we went on shore where there were several small cabins scattered around, and to one of those we went and obtained a few provisions. Our meals were not very regular, being a long ways apart. We obtained some cured fish and a few pounds of hard bread, and with this we were forced to get along with.

The valley is three and four miles wide all the way down, scattered at long intervals with clumps of live oaks; every little way could be seen droves of deer and antelope, and we saw one pack of grey wolves, the most numerous we had ever seen. Every little while Dan would say, "There they go! What a farming country this will be," Dan says: Yes, there is no finer land out doors than this same valley.

As we get farther down we begin to see attempts made towards fencing with wire; wire can be had, but the post material is scarce and hard to find; when they get a railroad they can then bring it from the Nevadas. There is an endless supply of all kinds of timber that will some day be very valuable.

The third day we arrived at the city, and lo! It was no more! having been burned up almost clean, and now it was overflowed, water and creek. We could see, as day began to break, a few half starved men rowing round in boats; how desolate everything looked! What a change from what it was when I was here last! Then could be heard throughout its entire length the hum of busy labor and the joyful sight of its happy people. It made us feel very sad, too, on our own account, as we thought to get work here, but nothing can be done until spring, and so the next morning we waded nearly out to Sutter's Fort before we could find dry land. I found the land all through here was largely fenced and under cultivation, not a sycamore tree could I see standing; in '49 they stood quite thick; all

In Search of Gold

in and around the city and Sutter's Fort it looks the same.

We now took our course for Weaver's Creek, some sixty miles beyond the foot hills. After leaving the valley no perceptible change had taken place. I pointed out the trees under which, two years before, I had taken such a cold; that night we camped under a large live oak and about midnight the rain that had been getting ready, now came down in torrents. The bough house we had made turned but little of the water and we were water soaked from head to foot; no more sleep until morning when we started on. About noon we came to what once was called "Sundown;" everything was changed except the eternal hills and water courses. King's rum shop was gone and in its place stood quite a respectable country store. We found on the site where Ross's boarding house stood once quite a respectable hotel; we went in and left our blankets and then went down to the Creek, but what a change! The very mountains had been washed away, and I could not find a single spot that I once knew; all was changed, and the little Lake they were pumping out to search for gold was gone; trees, ledges, dams, had all been removed in the search for gold. The entire Creek was now busy with Chinamen, the curse of the Pacific slope; they would work for a dollar a day and save money, and now these people were working it over again.

We soon found we could do nothing here and started across lots to Stockton, in the southern mines, some three hundred miles away; the rain came down almost every day. We now tried to get work, for my money was gone long ago, and Dan paid and said he would pay as long as it lasted, but his was nearly gone also. We began to live on one and sometimes two meals a day, and we could get nothing short of one dollar and a half a meal. We tried to find a place to mine and borrow tools, but all to no purpose, and it seemed as though the fates were entirely against our every effort, but we were not alone, for thousands of others were tramping around trying to keep up the spark of human life. All the cities, towns and camps along the rivers were overflowed, and all their stores destroyed; the whole mining region was overrun with thieves, gamblers and cut throats of every description under heaven.

Chapter XII

We continued to travel, and at last Dan's last dollar had fled beyond recall, and didn't we go hungry! [That] those that know it not may never know what hunger is, to go day after day with nothing to put in the stomach to keep it from collapsing; that terrible gnawing that comes from that repository, calling for food and will not be pacified. It seemed harder to stand the exposure of the elements, laying on the wet ground at night and wading the stream by day. Work, we could find none, it was the same old story; we can scarcely keep ourselves; who could blame them, we did not.

One night I said to Dan, "I think we can go on not more than one day more. The spirit is willing, but the flesh is getting very weak;" "yes," said Dan. Dan was no great talker and his sentences were very short; sometimes he seemed to be thinking, but if he did, he seldom expressed it in words, but they were no words of complaint.

The miners are now working the small gulches and light runs where there is more or less gold, and the dirt washes easy, and while it rains, can be shoveled without picking. In some places with a sluice, even with a small prospect to the pan, eight and ten dollars a day can be made. For about a hundred miles through here it is nearly all surface diggings; from two to four work in company. There are some gulches that prove very rich in pay dirt. At a place called "Montezuma Flats," that covered nearly a thousand acres, the surface some three feet deep, paid from six to ten dollars a day. Some of the small runs and depressions leading from the hills were very rich, taking out from two to three hundred dollars a day to the man.

CHAPTER XIII

Indian Bread — Cold, Wet and Hungry — A Friend in Time of Need — In Search of Work — The Stanislaus River — Cross the Ferry — Still on the Tramp — In the River — The Government Surveyors — Arrive at the "American House" — Its Landlord — A Wild Look — A Kind Friend — "Uncle John's Eating House" — Etc., Etc., Etc.

The fourth day from Weaver's Creek we came to a high mountain covered with live oaks, and here in a deep gulch we found a tribe of friendly Indians. To them we applied for something to eat, and they said lots of "Mericanas hungry." We said we were and presently the chief gave an order of some kind, and a squaw brought us some bread made of acorns; it did not taste very good to us, as hungry as we were. We asked them if there was any gold up the gulch worth digging. They said "No," but "away beyond the big mountain there was heaps of gold," but they have never been known to speak the truth on this or any other subject.

The next day we waded five considerable streams, having to take our clothes all off; this was cold work and laid the foundation for a system of rheumatics that was not laid down on my first chart of travels, but we must take whatever the gods may send. Said I, "Dan, how your teeth do chatter!" Alas, my own had caught the infection. Two of the streams were not more than a quarter of a mile apart, and we had to run up and down the bank to get warm before we tried the next.

Just before night we came to a ranch where they kept a kind of boarding house; we went in and warmed ourselves by the fire and the man says "You look cold," and he piled on more wood, "and your clothes are dripping wet," for it had been raining nearly all day. After standing by the fire some time he says, "Aren't you going to have some supper?" I said, "We would like some, but have nothing to pay with, but would like to earn it if you have anything we could do." He says, "Oh, well never mind that; come in and have some supper and we will see about that in the morning." This was a new phase to human nature that we had not met with before, so we went in and had a very nice supper; once in a while he came in and would say, "Don't be afraid, boys, eat all you want; you don't look as though you have had any too much lately." He gave us leave to lie down by the fire and sleep; this was a big change from sleeping outdoors on the wet ground in the rain.

The next morning we were up early and asked him if there was anything we could do. He said, "I will see after breakfast; so when breakfast was ready we went in and sat down with the rest of the family, and they were very nice folks; they had but a few boarders and what they did for a living I could not tell. After breakfast he gave us each an axe and showed us a large log and said we might cut that up into fire wood, which we did. He came out after awhile and said we might cut a few cords of wood and showed where to cut it; we worked three days and the fourth morning, after breakfast, he said, "Well, boys, you have worked well and here is twelve dollars, it will help you some; I did not care to have the wood cut, but to help you along a little." I thanked him kindly for his disinterested kindness to us, and he that presided over the destinies of men would repay him again fourfold; that in all our wandering through this land of gold we had found none so charitable as he. We now bid him goodbye and went on.

In Search of Gold

It was Sunday morning, the sun which had been obscured for many days now shone out in great splendor, and we said as we walked along we hoped our worst troubles were over, but alas, they had hardly began.

In four miles we came to a small ranch; this was aside from the mining district, and here seemed to be no gold for some distance, or at least there was no mining carried on here at this time. Here there had been some attempt at fencing by digging ditches, so we called at several ranches to get a job at ditching, but they said they done their work themselves and so we continued to travel day after day without finding anything to do. We had spread our resources out very thin, but now they were all gone.

We now came to the Stanislaus River and had but a single dollar left. The country here is very flat, and the most of it was overflowed at this time; on the opposite side of the river was a shanty, and we hallooed for some time, and at last a man came over in a boat. I said, "We would like to cross over; how much will you charge to take us over?" He said, "One dollar each." I said, "We have but one." "Well," he said, "you must stay where you are then," and he commenced to paddle back; he crossed over, fastened his boat and went into the shanty; in a few moments he came out again, got into the boat and came across. "Come, get in here, and I will try and get you over." The river was wide and the current swift, and Dan and I were obliged to lay down in the bottom of the boat; the man pulled a good stroke and we got across safe. We handed him the dollar and he said "Go in." We did so and found a man writing; he looked up and said, "You have but a dollar." I handed it to him and said, "I was in hopes to cross the river and have half a dollar left." He said, "I charge two dollars to those that have money to pay, but you shall have something to eat besides." So he took the dollar and gave us some dinner.

After dinner we started on. The valley is overflowed most of the way from here to Stockton, and all this day we tramped through water from one to three feet deep. Just before dark we came to a place where I could see no grass, and I said to Dan, "This must be a deep slough." Dan stopped and looked at it a moment and then said,

Chapter XIII

"I am going on, even if it is a river." He only took three steps when down he went souse all over; he could swim and got across. I thought, "How shall I get over; I cannot swim." When Dan went down he carried his blankets down too, and they were wet; my robe was done up snug and I threw it over as far as I could, and Dan in trying to catch it fell in again all over; he got out and sputtered considerable. Now our things were all wet. "Now," Dan says, "jump in and I will catch you when you come up." But I had made up my mind to slide in and then crawl on my hands until I reached the other bank. This I did according to programme, and arrived on the other side. The bottom was a sticky clay and at one time I thought I should stick there. Harry Gill's teeth never chattered half as fast as Dan's and mine did as we stood in the water on the other side; the night, too, was cold and very dark. We could see two distant lights and I said, "Come, Dan, let us lessen the distance between us and those lights as fast as possible." They appeared to be not more than a mile distant but were nearly three; we dreaded another slough, but could not have seen one if there had been, but by good luck we escaped them and went no deeper than our armpits.

At last we were out of the water and soon came to a shanty where we found a man and two women. They had moved out of Stockton, it being overflowed, and had just set up things so they could sleep; they were eating supper when we came up, and seeing how cold we were asked us to sit down and have some supper, but seeing that there was not enough for a cat we thanked them for the kind offer. The man said there were three houses in about two miles, but it was through water all the way, and the river run close by; that we must be careful and not get into it. We started out again, and the water not being much over two feet deep we arrived in about an hour alongside a house; into this we went without knocking. We were the coldest and wettest rats this side the Pacific slope; there was no one in at the time but there was a stove, however, and that we hugged, even if it was a stranger. Soon two men came in. I said as well as my chattering teeth would allow, "We are very cold, gentlemen." "That we can see," they said, and their man soon coming in they told him to make up a good fire so we could get warm; they asked us where

In Search of Gold

we came from and we told them. They said several men had been drowned in crossing where we had, and they congratulated us on making the passage on foot when others dared not try it on horseback. We talked there until nearly eleven, when they told us we had better go up overhead and spread our things down on the floor, which we did. We could not get warm, for we were chilled completely through. The man went up with us and covered us with a part of a tent; he then went down and in twenty minutes he returned with a bottle of brandy, and of this he made us drink quite a large quantity; he said if we did not we would be dead men before morning. Not being used to taking anything of the kind, in three minutes I knew no more until I heard some one asking if we were not going to have some breakfast. I said, "We have no money." "That makes no difference; come down and have some."

When we threw off our covering we were steaming like two hot potatoes and felt as well as ever. Their man told us they had sent out after the brandy, seeing how we were. He now showed us down into a long dining room where a table was set for sixteen; there was enough left now for that number, and the food was the very best. We found afterwards they were government surveyors. We now made a good square meal, for we knew not when we should get another.

When we had stowed away all we could with comfort, we tried to find some one to thank for their kindness, and though we hunted high and low we could find no one. I told Dan I thought it must be a place of enchantment for our especial benefit; we waited round for some time, but no one coming we went out into the town, which we found in a bad condition; by waiting we managed to reach what was called the "American House," and when we went in we looked like any miners from the mines with pockets full of the needful. We being wet and cold and wishing to get dry by the fire, I told Dan we must walk smart and take a chair by the stove, if there should be one, so we walked in like two millionaires, and sat down. A man came from behind the counter and said, "Gentlemen, let me take your bundles," which he did, saying, "Cold weather we are having." "Yes, quite," I said. "What news from the mines?" I said, "Plenty of

Chapter XIII

water now, and a very large amount of gold is being taken out." Dan could not keep from laughing, and the man looked a little closer and said no more. I thought he began to "smell a mice," and Dan taking it all in, hawhawed completely out; this showed the man he had been sold. We sat round the bar room until supper time, watching his method of doing business; when the bell rung, each man had a card for supper and then went in; after they were through, I said, "Dan, go up and ask him if we can have some supper." Dan said, "I'll be hanged if I do; the man looks now as if he could bite us in two." So I went up and said, "My friend, we are out of money just now, but we are in hopes to find work soon and then we can settle for a week's board." "That won't do; that is too thin; it's the same old story that hundreds have told me; the last few days a great many have slid in and got their meals for nothing and I shall feed no more without pay." "I can't blame you," I said; "I don't intend to get food for nothing. I am in hopes to get work and I can then pay." "No," he said, "You will get nothing here tonight." I said, "will you allow us to sleep on the floor tonight?" "No, I don't allow any one to sleep here but those that have their meals here." "Well," I said, "Will you allow us to leave our blankets here for a short time? If we do not return for them they are yours." "Well, yes," he said, "on those conditions, you can leave them." So we left them and went out and tried several places, but could get nothing. There had been so many in the same fix that the people had shut their doors and hearts against all that had no money; they were all young, smart and enterprising men, but were in this peculiar situation, and no way out of it, until the water goes down.

We travelled around until quite late, and we were afraid the hotel might be shut up. We had found a little outhouse where we proposed to sleep if no one else should get there before we did. We saw but a few tramps like ourselves. Dan said they had starved to death and been washed away by the flood; perhaps so, and it looked as though they might in a short time have company on that journey where the hungry are at rest.

We now went up and got our blankets and took up our quarters in the little outhouse. By this time it was raining hard and we were quite thankful to be under cover, but our stomachs gnawed so steadily on that we could sleep but little, and that little was disturbed by tantalizing dreams of an abundance of food just beyond our reach.

The next morning we started out again. Trying a new part of the town, travelling around all day; we could get neither food or work. Towards night we were standing on the corner of a street, and Dan was looking at me quite intently. I said, "What are you looking at me for?" He said, "You are looking wild; I hardly know you." "Well, Dan, I have noticed your face for some time, but thought it best to say nothing about it." As they were lighting up inside the house, I said, "Dan, I am going to take a new departure; I am going into that hardware store for something to eat; come." There was a dim light at the far end as I opened the door, and towards that light we went; there were two men in a small counting room, one was reading a paper; he looked up and said, "Good evening." I returned the salutation and then said, "It would seem that people must starve here in your city." "How, what do you mean?" "I mean that we have travelled all over this place and at almost every house have tried to get work and something to eat, but have failed in every case. We have not had anything pass our lips but a little water from the river for two days." He held the lamp up to our faces and said, "This is too bad! I knew this overflow had thrown a great many out of house and home and any way of getting a living, but have seen nothing like this. Come with me." He led the way out and down a short street into an eating house. Going up to the proprietor and pointing to us, said, "Give these two men a good supper and lodging and I will settle with you in the morning;" he then bid us good evening and went out. The man set before us some odds and ends of bread and meat, and this soon vanished. Knowing our charitable friend would be charged for a full meal, I, like Oliver Twist, called for more, and he brought on some more and then said, "That is all you will get tonight, and more than you ought to have." Dan tried to speak, but his mouth being full he lost more than he gained. When everything was disposed of we spread our blankets and were soon sound asleep, freed from the thoughts of the morrow.

Chapter XIII

By the first dawn of day we were up and out on the street; the water had fallen very fast during the night and things began to look brighter. We went up the street, on the water front, and on a sign over a door I read "Uncle John's Eating House;" that seemed to sound clever. Said I, "Dan, let us go in here; I don't think the old gentleman was in when we came here yesterday." We went in and I saw an old man by the stove cooking. I said, "Good morning, Uncle John; you are up early this morning." "Yes," he said, "that boy of mine likes to sleep in the morning." Said I, "Uncle John (and he looked like a man that any one might be happy to have for an uncle,) I may want to get a few meals here. We have no money at present, but I am in hopes to get work soon, as the water is going down fast, and when I do, I will pay for all we have." "Very well," he said, "you look like honest men and I will trust you. I have fed a great many and they have failed to put in an appearance afterwards, and if you can find a place not occupied, spread your blankets here nights." This kindness gave us great relief.

We went out and walked around all day, but nothing turned up to our advantage. Dan thought we ought to have had our breakfast and dinner, but I said, which we went without, for I wished to put off the inevitable as long as possible. As soon as the place was lit up we went in and got some supper. Said I, "Uncle John, we have found nothing yet, but have been on the lookout all day; don't be discouraged." He said, "We don't know what the morrow will bring forth."

CHAPTER XIV

The Gambling House — French Camp — Hungry and no Work — The Generous Captain — Start Again for the Mines — The Valley of the San Joaquin — Attacked by Robbers — "Food for Man and Beast" — Tuolumne County — Chinese Camp — Mining — Etc., Etc., Etc.

After supper we went out on the street, and hearing music we went up a few doors and found it came from a gambling house on quite a large scale. The place was quite full, and several games of chance were going on, money was changing hands quite fast, most generally into the hands of the banker. I saw one man lose his all and then borrow a quarter of a dollar of a friend; he won and then continued to double it until he had eight hundred dollars in gold and silver piled up before him, then his luck changed and he lost all, even the borrowed quarter.

As we stood there looking on, a man touched me on the shoulder and said, "Want a job?" I said, "I do." "Then come here at eleven o'clock tonight and I will tell you what to do." I said, "There are two of us." "All the better, it will be sooner done." We now went back to Uncle John's and stayed until the time set to be there. I said,

Chapter XIV

"Uncle John, I have been promised a small job at eleven o'clock tonight. Perhaps you will be shut up before we get through." "No," he said, "I never fasten up; you can come in at any time when you get through." At eleven sharp we were on hand; there were a few there yet, but soon went away. The doors were now closed and the man brought us two mops and two pails, and said he wanted the floor scrubbed up clean. He said, "I shall pay you a dollar an hour." We went to work and cleaned the place up in good shape in two hours and went back to our blankets with lighter hearts than for a long time. We had earned enough to pay breakfast with Uncle John and paid him our four silver dollars. He looked up and said, "I was not mistaken when I said you were honest and would pay. Now come in and get your regular meals; you went without yesterday all day; don't do that again while Uncle John can give you a meal of victuals."

After breakfast we went out and crossed the river where a small vessel was loading. I asked the captain where he was bound to and he said, "French Camp." I said, "Do you think there would be any show there for us, in the shape of work?" He said, "The show for work anywhere at this time is very slim, but you can try; you can work your passage up with me;" so we went up to French Camp. We helped the captain unload; he then said, "I shall be up here again day after tomorrow, and if you do not get work I will take you back again." We then started up to the small settlement and made the rounds long before night, with our usual bad luck. We got nothing to eat that day, and at night we got permission to spread our blankets on the floor.

The next morning we heard there was a man that wanted some ditching done, out some four miles from here, so we started, and the man said "It is too wet to dig at this time and besides, I have nothing to pay with." I asked him if he could give us a mouthful of food; he said he wished he could, but his own stores were very short, he had a wife and four children. I thought perhaps they might become more hungry than ourselves.

We then started back and arrived about dark at the Camp. This was the second day without anything to eat, and the captain would not be up until ten or eleven the next forenoon. Said I, "Dan, this is a long fast." "Yes," said Dan, "now let us go down to the other hotel; there are women folks there. We will go around to the back door and if we can see one of them perhaps they will give us enough to keep us until the captain comes up." So we went down and as bad luck would have it, I came to the door just as a woman did. She thought I was a robber and gave an awful scream and we had to take to our heels. We did not think it best to go there again and so came around to the front and went in; they could give us nothing to eat, but we obtained leave to sleep on the floor; we slept but little.

The next morning we went down to the landing to wait for the Captain, and as we were not feeling very well, the want of food had a very depressing effect on our minds.

At ten the vessel came to the landing and we helped unload and then started on the return. The Captain asked us how we made out. I told him it was the third day and we had had nothing to eat. "What," said he, "haven't you had anything since you left the city?" I said, "No, we have not." "Here is my dinner, a loaf of bread and some cheese; you must be nearly famished." "Yes," said Dan. The captain's dinner was soon disposed of and it gave us some relief, and were in hopes to get in before the shops were shut up, but having a head wind we did not arrive until eleven o'clock at night.

The next morning we had some breakfast and went out to the river. The Captain came along and said, "I want to hire one of you for a month, and will pay you sixty dollars." I said, "Have you any choice, captain?" He said, "No." Then I said, "Dan is your man;" but Dan wanted me to take it. "No," I said, "I can do battle with the world much better than you can," and so it was decided that Dan should go with the Captain, and I should do the best I could.

As we were talking the matter over a man came along and said, "Did you ever work in the mines?" I said I had a good deal. He says, "I have just come from the mines, and not knowing anything about mining I could make nothing; but if I had some one that knew, we could do well enough." "Well," I said, "I would like to try it with you, but I have no funds at present and owe Uncle John for my breakfast." "Well," he says, "I have some, enough, I think, for what

Chapter XIV

we shall want, and when you get the money you can pay it back." Then I said, "I am your man." We now bought a tin pan, frying pan, a few tools and some provisions, and the next morning, after settling up with Uncle John, and bidding Dan goodbye, I was not thinking that it was the last time I should see him, but it proved to be so. "Now," I said, "Dan, be good, and I will write to you shortly how I get on." Dan wanted to go with us, but the Captain held him to the bargain, and we started on, and a little before night, arrived at the Lone Tent, some two miles from anywhere.

The Valley of the San Joaquin, at this place, is very wide, and will some time make a fine farming country. We had baker's bread and some salt beef, so all we wanted was a place to sleep; the tent was oblong and twelve feet wide, so when it came bed time, by mutual consent, we lay down with our feet to each other, thus making two rows of men twenty-five feet long and twelve feet wide. There being but one door what traffic there was must pass over our feet. Two men had occasion to leave the tent hurriedly during the night, and this brought them over our feet on the double quick; some used very bad words as their boots took the skin off in large flakes. We were awakened several times during the night.

The next morning we started on before any of the rest were up, and about eight we stopped and made some coffee and with our baker's loaf we made a hearty meal. We then went on until almost dark, when we found a bunch of live oaks, and under these we made our camp by cutting some branches of chaparral brush. These we set up around and some on the top, and in this way we made it quite comfortable.

After getting supper we sat down by the fire, and I commenced to tell Solon, my companion, of how Dan and I had travelled through the country, of our cold, wet and hungry tramp of five hundred miles, how much we had suffered, when up rode two greasers (Mexicans) and said, "Your money or we will blow you into __ __." We both jumped up and my companion jerked out a revolver. I had no idea he had one, and he blazed away, and as good luck would have it tumbled one from his horse; the other I was throwing brands of fire at, blinding his aim, so he done no damage. When his companion fell, he put spurs to his horse and fled, Solon firing his last charge after him, but with no perceptible effect. The robber that lay on the ground, entangled in his accoutrements, his horse trying to get away, was quite a novel sight to us. We soon had the horse secured. We then examined the wounded robber and found the ball had passed through his shoulder, and the man said it pained him (carambo); what to do with him we did not know. Solon said, "Let us hang him to yonder that tree." "It would serve him right." I said, "But there are organized courts in the land. Now we must take him along to Montezuma and leave him with the proper authorities; but we can do nothing more tonight; we must fasten this one up and one of us must watch until midnight and the other until day; we must also keep our eyes peeled, for the other one may return and give us a shot."

Everything now being arranged we put out the fire and Solon lay down and tried to get some sleep. While I stood guard I examined the robber's outfit and found a brace of horse pistols; one was empty, the other I kept in my hand in case of emergency, the Mexican eying me the while; a serape or blanket, two knives and a pack of dirty cards.

At twelve, or as near as I could guess, as it was cloudy, I called Solon. How quick he jumped up! He said he had a horrid dream, and now was glad it was but a dream. I gave him the robber's pistol, and charged him to be vigilant. I then lay down, and being tired, having travelled all day, was soon sound asleep. It was nearly day when I awoke, and Solon was starting a fire to get breakfast; the robber complained of his shoulder, for it had swollen a great deal. We got some cold water and were about to bathe it when he said, "Put on some whiskey." We examined his coat and found a small flask and bathed the wound; it must have been pretty sore for he kept saying "Carambo;" our sympathy was not such as it would have been under other circumstances.

After eating our breakfast and binding the robber on the horse we started on, Solon leading the horse and I bringing up the rear. We continued to travel in this way for nearly three hours, when we came to a small camp; here there happened to be a constable. To

Chapter XIV

him we delivered our prisoner. We told him we should claim the horse and saddle as the spoils of victory; he said he would get us an order on the high sheriff at Sonora which he did, and he went off with the prisoner; we were glad to get rid of such bad company.

We travelled on until after dark when we came to a shanty, and over the door it read "Food for man and beast." We went in; the place was so full the man said he could not keep us, but three miles farther there was a public house kept by one Shaw so we started on. We were very tired, and the night being dark it seemed a long road. At last we arrived, they were just going to shut up house. One of the proprietors I knew, he was one of the company that came out in the New Jersey in '49; we sat up quite late, talking of the various scenes each had passed through. The next morning we started on, our supper, lodging and breakfast costing us but a small sum. This kindness we were very thankful to receive. From here to Montezuma flats is eight miles; this was the point we had started for. At Shaw's we strike the Six-Bit Gulch; at noon we arrived at the flat and left our blankets at an eating house kept by one Snow. I asked him what he charged for board a week. He said twenty dollars. I said, "I have no money, but I am going to try and dig some out." "All right," he said, "when you get it you can pay." Here was an opening at last. We went out prospecting for two days but could find nothing that would pay. The next day a man offered Solon five dollars a day to work for him a week. He asked me if he should go. I said, "Yes, by all means go and earn all you can; that is very good pay for the times," so the next morning he went.

I went prospecting all day, found a few claims that would pay, and marked them off. Every diggings has its own laws; here it was twelve feet square and as many as you could dig around a foot deep, with the name of the man so claiming posted for one week. This held, but if the claim proved very rich and lawless men should come that way, you must fight to hold it, and in many cases the strongest party took possession and kept it until some other party stronger came along, then they were ousted out.

The next day I heard of a man who wanted some ditching done. I went down and made a bargain to work for a month at sixty dollars. I went and got my robe, and the next mooring I went to work. The ranch was owned by three partners, George and Charles [and Manning]. Charles was at work in Stockton at the time; the ranch contained six hundred and forty acres, and was on the main road from Sonora to Stockton. George also kept a public house; the house was a curious one but answered every purpose for which it was required. The next morning I went to work throwing up dirt for a fence; George intended to enclose eighty acres. I worked here for nearly a month; one morning we found an ox nearly worn out, and George having one of his own we made a yoke and with this team we hauled some timber for fencing. Some of the land was quite good in the runs and small valleys, and on the hills and among the trees red clover grew quite stout, making nice hay; we cut some hay early in the runs for teams that stopped here over night. The land all through Tuolumne County is quite red in color, and in some parts a gravelly loam. Good barley can be raised on most of it; they commence to plow and sow as soon as the rainy season sets in, about the first of November.

George not having but little money he said he would like to have me take half of the stock of provisions as part pay and so divide the profits of keeping public house. This went on for a while quite well, but as the season advanced trade fell off fast so that it did not pay. I said to George, "Let us go over the mountain on to Six-Bit Gulch." He did not believe it would pay, but was willing to try, so the 15th of March we took with us a few tools and crossed the mountain about three miles travel. The water was very high at this time so that only the edge of the stream could be worked; we found some quite good prospects during the day, so much so that we concluded to purchase a tom and tools. We went that day to look at one that lay up the gulch about a mile; this we bought for eight dollars, quite a good one; it belonged to Shaw that kept the stage house where they changed horses. He took it for debt and was glad to get rid of it.

The next day we started early for the gulch. Shaw let us have his team to haul the tom down to our claim; we had got all ready to go to work, but lacked a hose to conduct the water into the tom. In the afternoon we went to Chinese Camp, about two miles from the gulch; this was quite a place, a large extent of surface that paid well for washing. Here we bought some duck and the next day made it up. We were now ready to commence operations, so early the next morning, instead of going by the road which was considerable farther, we cut a path over the mountain; this took until nearly noon, the rest of the day we worked washing; at night we had four dollars; this was not very encouraging, but much better than keeping house.

The next day being Sunday we did not work, but went up to Montezuma and paid my indebtedness to Snow and Solon that I had not seen since leaving him. He and another man were about leaving for Silver Creek; they tried to induce me to go with them, but I did not intend to start out again while the rainy season lasted, I had seen enough of that. I bid Solon goodbye and told him to remember those two Mexican robbers. He said, "I shall ever remember that sharp skirmish of that evening, and that firebrand you worked in to such good purpose." I had not heard from the captured robber since we gave him up to the constable. I still held the papers he had given us for the horse; I had forgotten to mention this to Solon, perhaps he may come back again before I leave this place.

The next Monday morning we went down to the gulch. It commenced to rain about the time we got to work; I never saw it rain much harder, but we kept at work, but soon found the water rising fast, so fast in fact we were obliged to carry our tom and tools up above high water mark. We now started back; to say we were wet would not express but little of the condition we were in. When we arrived home we found an eight mule team waiting to be put up.

The next morning we tried it again, the water having gone down we went to work, and at night we found our day's work weighed eight dollars. This was not great, but encouraging when the water should get down. We worked this way until the first of April, some days making five dollars each. George's brother Charles came on the tapis now. He said hay baled up would bring where it was one hundred dollars a ton, and he had been through the hills and said there was a good crop, and more money could be made that way than mining. They concluded to try it on, but I told them I would continue mining; I was not so sanguine of the hay enterprise. We all three worked mining for a few days, when we moved our tent and what we had down to the gulch and set our tent up under some large sugar pines quite near the gulch.

The rainy season had now passed, and the water that had been high all along went down fast. In a few days the brothers went into the hills making hay and I was left alone; this was dull work for some time, but after awhile I became used to it.

Old Doctor Sears was at work down the gulch with six hired men; he said he claimed a mile of the gulch; he claimed so much for each man, and that I was at work on his claim. After he and his men had gone down to work I went up to Shaw's and asked Lawrence, Shaw's partner in the concern, what the laws were on the gulch. He said each man could claim one hundred feet from shore to shore and lengthways of the stream. He then wrote two notices that John Fisk & Co. claimed three hundred feet. I now got two stakes and fastened them three hundred feet apart with the notice on each; when the Doctor and his men returned at night he saw the claim had been laid out according to law. He was very wrathy and said he would do this and that if I did not leave. I took no notice of him but kept at work.

CHAPTER XV

My Experience in the Mines — The Panther — Build a Stockade — A New Arrival — Melons and Cucumbers — Baked Beans — A Surprise — The Good Book and its Effects — "Cleaning out the Tom" — Sell the Claim — Prospecting for a New Claim — Build a Log Cabin — The Stage Driver — A Sudden Departure — The Rainy Season — George and the Grizzly — Prospecting the Island — Etc., Etc., Etc.

The third day after the boys had left me, I made seven dollars a day. The next day four miners came and took a prospect below my claim; they thought it would pay if a dam was built and the water turned off. I said I was willing to take hold and help; this seemed to be for my especial benefit, in two days we had the water turned and they went to work and worked for two days, and it not paying them what they had expected, they threw up their claim and left for parts unknown.

Building the dam was a good thing for me. The next day I made eight dollars, and here I worked all alone for five months. George coming down occasionally to see me and know how I got on. I tried to find out how they were making it in the hills; they could not tell

In Search of Gold

until it was sold, and that would not be until October, when the hay harvest would be over.

I went up to Chinese Camp and bought a week's provision, such as salt pork, bacon, flour, candles, molasses, beans, and some other things that were necessary for one that was working hard. These things were packed down to the tent on a mule free of charge, there being considerable opposition in the place.

In May I could dig in the middle of the gulch, the water had got down so low, and now I had my breakfast just as the sun was rising every morning that I might do the hardest work before it became too hot where I was at work. I threw off six feet of the top and washing about six inches; this was clay and soft ledge; the gold could be seen in this, it was so fine and in flat scales and very pure, without any quartz rock mixed with it. Six feet long and four feet wide was all I could do in a day. Four of the best days work I done here was twenty-five dollars a day. After I threw the dirt off down to the pay dirt, the water came in so fast that two buckets of dirt was all I could get out before I must bail the hole out again; this was hot and hard work. I could work no longer than ten in the forenoon, then commence at three in the afternoon and work until the hole was worked out. The days were very long in June, some seventeen hours; this made a long day.

One of the stage horses died and was hauled down within half a mile of my place, and this brought the wild animals around. One night I was awakened by the scream of a panther; it was a bright moonlight night, and the scream was so near it gave me a severe start; I could feel my hair starting up on my head, and at one time I thought my scalp would leave without further notice. I had nothing to defend myself with but a small hatchet, and this I had in my berth. In a few moments I could see the shadow of the panther through the canvas as he went smelling around the tent. He snuffed under the edge of the canvas at one place, and I thought he would come in sure. I had some salt fish and smoked salmon; they smelled strong and I thought he smelled them, and I wished it all at the bottom of the Red Sea. He nosed round there for some time and then I heard another animal coming down the gulch. It sounded like a bull with a bad cold. The panther seemed to move off, and I could not see his shadow any longer, but could hear the other animal yell, and the sound came nearer every moment. In about five minutes the panther gave a most horrid scream and the other animal too; they had evidently clinched. What a noise and crashing among the chaparral they did make! I sat up for a long time listening to the fight, but at last all was still, and after listening some time longer and hearing nothing more I lay down and after awhile went to sleep.

When I awoke the next morning the sun was shining through a hole in the canvass. I was soon up, had breakfast and went out to view the place where the animal contest had been, and there I saw blood and hair; the ground was torn up fearfully; they must have both got off as I could not see or hear either. I thought if this is the sort of company that I am to have, I must have something better than canvas for protection against them; so after breakfast I got an ax and cut stakes enough to make a stockade around the tent five feet high and as close together as I could set them. This required a good deal of hard labor, and it was nearly four days before I had it finished. The door I made of cross pieces pinned together, and on the inside I had a heavy brace that I could use in case of need.

The fourth night I slept in quiet security, but I could hear the animals quarreling for several nights over the old horse, but they troubled me no more at this time.

About this time a man came and set up his tent not far from me. His name was Jones, and he said he had run away from school; his home was in South Carolina, and his father had placed him at school in New York. He took the gold fever and came to the mines; he said he was studying for the law; he was a hard looking chap at this time; he had been into everything he could get into and come out alive. He took up a claim half a mile down the creek where he would work about three days and then go off up to Sonora and be gone a week or more. He read a good many novels that did him but little good, and he said he had two books he had just borrowed; they were about ghosts and must be read between eleven and twelve at night. He said one night he was reading according to programme, when he heard a noise and looked around and saw the toes of a pair of boots sticking through under the canvas, and he thought it was a man standing there certain, he was never more frightened; the story was very scary besides. He was one of those men that seem to be of little use to the world.

There was an island in the gulch containing about half an acre of made land, and would require but little labor to prepare it for planting, so George and I went to work one day that he came down, and dug part of it over and planted watermelons and cucumbers, then fenced it with brush to keep out Shaw's cows that sometimes came down the gulch to feed on the water weeds that grew near the margin of the stream. He kept about a dozen and sold the milk at Chinese Camp at fifty cents a quart. Our melons and cucumbers came up nicely and grew nights while I was asleep, being on a low island the ground was moist and the great heat of the sun made them grow very fast; how full those vines did set with fruit!

Every day, except Sundays, I worked on my claim it paying very well. Sundays I always had baked beans. I went into the tent to get something, I don't remember what, but as I turned round I saw a small book lay on the table; it was not there when I was in a few moments before, that I am quite certain of, and no one had been there for more than a month. I thought this very singular. I took the book up and read it through before going out to look after my beans. The book related to the Crucifixion of our Saviour; the scene was so effectingly portrayed that I was very much impressed, and here in this lone solitude, by these tall pines, I received that knowledge which is so necessary to the salvation for man, and never has it left me from that day to the present time, and in all my wanderings over the earth it has kept me from falling.

September had come and George came down; he said they had done haying and wanted to go to mining. I had quite recently bought a claim of Jones for fifty dollars and had worked there but two days; it paid nearly as well as the old one; so George took one-half the cost and we went to work. I could see that we had struck a good lead, the upper riffle sparkled with gold. I told George it was paying well, and he shoveled harder than ever. At noon I said we had better wash out and take the gold with us. George looked at the rifle and said, "Let it be; we won't wash out until night for it will seem so much more to take out." I did not like to leave it, for there might some one come along, although there seldom did, so we went up and got dinner and when we came back I saw Jones going down the gulch. I said, "George, Jones has cleaned out our tom." Oh no, he thought not. When we came there the dirt that contained the gold had been taken out and more dirt put in, minus the gold, thinking we would go to work without looking in underneath, George felt very bad. "There," said he, "Just my luck; if I had not said anything we should have our gold now," about fifteen dollars we thought. "Now," he says, "don't pay any attention to me after this, but go ahead." Jones came around a few days afterwards and I asked him how much gold he found in our tom the other day, and he denied all knowledge of it whatever; he wanted to know if I charged him with it. I said he was the only scape-grace that was around here, according to his own statements. However, we could prove nothing and said no more about it.

We worked the claim out, and one day he came along and wanted to know what we would sell him the claim back for. I said, "Twenty dollars." He said, "Here is your money." He told us afterwards he did not get but eight dollars and worked four days, and we thought it served him right.

We now went to work and finished working out the old claim. We had been having cucumbers and melons in great abundance and wished we had planted some potatoes and sweet corn, they are so nice in their season. Charles having disposed of the hay crop, came down and went to work with me. He said Manning, the third owner in their ranch, wanted to sell his share, and he thought it would be a good investment if I would like it. In a few days Manning came and I bought him out.

Soon after we went prospecting for a new claim, and up the gulch neatly opposite the stage house I found a very good prospect. We worked here about a week, and not paying more than six dollars a day each and having a chance to sell it for one hundred dollars I let it go.

We now went up the gulch still farther and prospected, but found nothing until we came to a large claim worked by a man by the name of Lamson. He had four men to work for him. We found a small claim that had been marked off, and I got a good prospect here, one I thought would pay quite well. We bought this for one hundred dollars. We had been at work here about three weeks when Lamson came to us one day and offered to sell the whole claim, tent, tom, sluices, in fact everything on the claim, for six hundred dollars, and we might have three days to prospect and make up our minds. We went to work and found the prospect so good as to warrant our making an offer of the price asked, but he was to leave as soon as the money should be paid. I said this will be two hundred each; they said that they had nothing to pay with. I said, "Where is the money you got for the hay?" They had not got anything for it yet, but were in hopes to get their money the first of November; but the first of November never brought their money; they were swindled out of the whole. This was a serious lull, but still their courage was pretty good. I paid Lamson for the claim the next day and he left. The understanding between us was that I should be treasurer and keep the bank until their part was paid. They were as nice fellows as any one could wish to have for partners.

We now had work enough to last all winter and more, so we concluded to build a cabin on the site of our old tent, under the tall pines. A man by the name of Stubblefield that had hired our ranch, had six yoke of oxen that he had come across the Plains with, and we hired a yoke of steers of him to draw the logs down the mountain; two of us cut and the other drove team. In two days we had enough for the purpose. The next four days we put it up, covering the top with the tent; this made us a good house. We had a fireplace at one end and the door at the other. We put up some berths that would be comfortable, and thus we were fixed for winter quarters. We laid in provisions for three months, for they are much higher after the rain season sets in, for then everything must be packed on mules or jacks.

We commenced on our new claim where Lamson left off and made very fair pay. We struck a new lead and followed it; it lead under the stage road. One day as we got through on the other side of the road the stage came down from Sonora, drawn by four horses; the driver, when he had driven across, stopped and came back with his long whip. He wanted to know if we wanted to let the stage down in that hole? He did not wait for an answer, but said if we did not begin to fill that hole up in three minutes he would lay the whip over our heads. Five or six men stuck their heads out of the stage. We were down some six feet, and I ran to where I could get out, and as soon as I got on the bank I threw down my hat and run my hand into my shirt bosom as if to draw a revolver, and walked towards him and said, "Another word and you are a corpse!" It was all that was needed. He got on directly and drove off. Said Charles, "Have you got a revolver?" "No, I have not." If one had been passing at this time they might have heard a roar of laughter that made the welkin ring, and the incident was referred to long afterwards with merriment. We were going to fill up each side of the road, and the next day we made it all safe as before.

This lead went a few rods farther and then terminated in a very thin stratum of clay that did not pay to throw the surface off. We prospected to find and pick up the lead again, but were unsuccessful. We now commenced back and took another strip of twelve feet wide, which paid about seven dollars a day to each man. This paid for digging quite well.

The second of November the rainy season set in, and for many days we could do nothing but sit by the fire and read or mend our clothes. Our claim was some distance from the cabin and many was the ducking we got that winter, but every chance that we could get we were at work. In about a month the brothers paid up for their part of the claim; the claim continued to pay about the same all winter.

One day along in March another stage horse had died and they had hauled it down very near where the other had been and about a week after George had occasion to go up to Shaw's after dark, and coming back by the old horse there was Mr. Grizzly at work getting his supper. George not seeing him until quite near, and the bear not liking to be disturbed took after George on the full jump. George threw open his safety valve and putting on all the steam he had kept ahead and came into the cabin without knocking. Did he look pale? Well, yes, not only pale but frightened from stem to stern; it was some time before he could speak and tell us what had taken place to disturb him so.

The next morning we saw the tracks of the bear; he had followed George to within two rods of the cabin, but George's tracks were the longest apart of any we had ever seen.

I had written to Dan some time ago but had heard nothing from him. There was a man going to Stockton and I sent word by him. He said he could hear nothing of him. I wanted to pay him the money he had paid out for me on our starvation tramp, which neither of us will ever forget.

March has come at last, bringing with it the blossoming of the Lord's flower garden; the whole earth is covered with blossoms of every color and shade. This is a great relief—these three weeks of blossoms. Then in April the chaparral and other shrubs take their turn; then the red clover among the hills are in all their glory.

We now thought we would prospect the island on our claim. We found a large round hole that had been dug nearly two years before, some six feet deep. I said, "Boys, I am going into that hole and take a prospect." They did not believe I should find anything. I found the bottom of the hole was on the bed rock, and I picked up a pan full and washing it out, getting six bits or seventy-five cents. This was much better than we had expected. George had taken one at the same time on the edge of the dirt. Here was an opening for work for a long time; all hands would turn to and throw off the surface in the forenoon and wash the gold from the dirt, it being composed of part clay and rotten ledge, in the afternoon. The second day Charles picked up a small nugget that weighed eighteen dollars; there was considerable quartz rock mixed in it, with a very rough surface, and not a handsome specimen by any means. Charles said he must carry that home to show to his mother.

CHAPTER XVI

Working out the Road Tax — Sonora — Hydraulic Mining — Surface Mining — "Spirit Hollow" — "I am Free! I am Free!" — Music and Gambling — Sunday in the Mines — Use of Quicksilver in Mining — Poison Oak — The Fox and the Rooster — An Unwelcome Visitor — The Alarm Signal — A Visit to Chinese Camp — Wood's Creek — Poverty Flat — Etc., Etc., Etc.

We found several small pieces that were quite pure. In washing away this island it occupied us until June, when Shaw, the highway surveyor, came and notified us we must work out our road tax of five dollars each. The next morning about twenty of us met in his place, the stagehouse, and after treating us all round we started on up the road, throwing in a shovel full here and there, throwing out a few stones and stopping to tell a story. This occupied more time than all the rest; all the forenoon was wasted in this manner. We arrived back again about eleven o'clock, and he says, "Come, boys, this is dry work," and he gave us another treat. "Now, boys," he says, "go home; your tax is worked out." The Chinese did not come off so easy; there was a money tax and taxed twice a year.

In Search of Gold

The next Saturday we all three went up to Sonora, sixteen miles. We started early, before day, that we might get there in season to see the sights and hear the sounds. We came to a place where there was hydraulic mining, the water coming from a height of one hundred and fifty feet, coming through a small nozzle like a fire engine. This has a tremendous power and eats into the hardest dirt formation with great rapidity. If the dirt will yield the color to the pan it will pay very well; here a mountain had been nearly washed away. Further on were surface diggings where only a foot is washed.

Three miles beyond this is a large surface of country busy with miners working with water brought in flumes a long distance, taken from a river. This is an enterprise of itself and requires capital. Every man using water pays so much a day, according to the quantity used. This is a very busy scene, and it has but recently been opened, and for a long distance the miners could be seen at their work; they made from six to eight dollars a day after paying for the use of water. Here the earth is composed largely of quartz rock, in small pebbles. I told George I thought gold would be found to pay better some time, deep down.

In the middle mines, at this time, we heard they had gone through the first bed rock and found large quantities of gold near the second; also came the excitement about Gold Lake, sixty miles to the East of Feather River, and this started off a large number of miners that were doing well. The story was that a man had found a lump of gold he could not lift, or carry; neither would he hire any one to help him, and there he sat on the golden boulder until he, poor man, fell off and died. The way of it was, so we afterwards heard, that a man having a large quantity of provisions on hand had them teamed to this distant place and then started this story to get miners there that he might sell at a great price. The enterprise worked well at first, but the man lost his life, having been murdered for his money.

The day being pleasant and not very hot, we wandered around among the mines getting what information we could; this being our day out, we meant to enjoy it the best we could.

At one place called Stepping Stones, they told us of Spirit Hol-

Chapter XVI

low, some two miles out of our way. They said a murder had been committed there a year ago near a flat stone composed of quartz, and any one standing on that rock, at evening time, would be touched on the shoulder by an unseen hand. We having the curiosity to see the place, started that way and arrived about nightfall; the stone was quite visible from the edge of the hollow some sixty feet off; there was not a breath of air stirring at the time. Charles says that near that stone most likely the man was murdered. We could see nothing about the place that would seem so very scary after all we had heard. I said, "George, go and stand on that stone and be touched." "No, not I." "Well, Charles, you go and try it on." He had rather be excused. "What, coming all this distance and not test the truth of the thing; then I must go." I started, went across, stepped on the stone and was turning around to return, when I felt some one touch me on the shoulder; the touch seemed to penetrate to the very marrow of my bones. I tried to open my lips to yell, but could not. I could feel my hair had taken a rise without any aid from me. I could hear a far off voice and yet it seemed quite near. "I am free! I am free!" then I felt myself at liberty to move and not before. I stepped off the stone and was soon beside the brothers.

It takes some time to tell all this, but it occurred not more than three moments. As I stood beside them George said, "How you tremble, and how pale you are!" Said I, "Don't look any more pale than you do." They said they felt a kind of fear they could not describe; they heard the voice say, "I am free," and it made them shiver.

We now walked away as fast as possible and arrived in Sonora about seven, went to a saloon and had supper, then went into a gambling saloon to hear the music which was very good, stopped and looked on and saw them play. We then went out and across to the Palace, looked that over and saw some of their fancy images, nice to look at, but not to touch. Then George wanted to see the Chinese wax figures; this occupied another half hour. We then found a lodging house and went to bed, pretty well tired out.

The next morning we were up early and walking about the place. We were the only ones about for a long time; the place is mostly

In Search of Gold

built of canvas, like most other mining camps, the gambling element taking the lead, and a great deal of gold changes hands in a short time. One miner came in from the mines with five thousand dollars and they got it all away in one night. The next morning he went back to work again and worked three years, when he came down again with about the same amount. He was perfectly sober this time, although he appeared to have been drinking; he came in and staggered up to a monte bank and threw down five thousand dollars in gold dust, saying, "Here's for the States or the mines; I don't care which." He had four companions that stood in the back ground; in case of any trouble they could step to the front. They let him win, thinking he had more; he took the gold and said, "Now for the States!" and started out. The gambler said, "Not so fast," and drew his revolver; the man's companions now stepped forward and said, "Now sit down and keep still." This was a story told for a fact; that is all that I know about it.

Sunday is the grand harvest day of the week; the miners shell out this day freely to the gaming tables, bull and bear fights among the Spanish and Mexican people, cockfights and rum fights without number, and the days go on. Charles bought him an accordion; George bought an octave flute, I bought a flute also. We then started for home and arrived about dark. We left the cabin and moved up on the claim in Lamson's old tent that had been standing all this time unoccupied. We bought five hens and a white rooster, for which we paid fifteen dollars, and we made a nice little house for them to roost and lay in; we fed them on barley mostly. I never had hens lay any better than they did; eggs sold for seventy-five cents a dozen. But we ate the most of them, selling only enough to buy their grain.

We now sold our ranch to Stubblefield, taking part money and the balance in stock; this we drove down to Samson Valley to fatten them up for suitable beef. Every day while it was too hot to work, Charles gave us a lesson in music, and after a few weeks we could play a few tunes quite well; this was quite a relief from hard work.

The gold being fine where we are now at work, we thought per-

Chapter XVI

haps some went over the riffle and was lost, so we bought eight pounds of quicksilver for eight dollars and had a box made to put it in, four inches wide, four inches deep, and sixteen inches long. This box was placed under the sand board and all the dirt and gravel dropped into it, but did not stay there, but passed out, the gold being heavier than the silver, settled into it and held it. Every Saturday night the quicksilver was strained through a piece of canvas and then run as dry as possible; this left a small cake, gold and quicksilver, the gold being coated with silver. This cake is placed on an iron shovel and held over a hot fire until the silver is burned off; this cements the gold together and oftentimes makes quite pretty specimens. There being some quicksilver mixed with it, it sells a dollar an ounce less than the other. The gold we dug from the island sold for eighteen dollars an ounce; but most of the gold is sold for seventeen dollars the ounce, and the quicksilver for sixteen dollars. We got most generally from a week's washing between seven and eight dollars; this was a good investment.

June days were now on the tapis and short nights were the order. What hot days they were! But the nights were quite cool, so we could sleep quite well. There were but two hot nights this season.

We now got hold of some poison oak, not knowing anything of it, and there being quite a lot where we were at work, and the first intimation we had was we could not open our eyes. The next morning how the flesh did burn and itch! As good luck would have it, Charles was not so badly poisoned but he could see, and a man that came round with milk said if we could find the "soap onion" and make suds of that and bathe the parts several times a day, we should soon get relief. Charles soon found the plant down in the gulch, quite near the poison oak; it was remarkable how soon it gave relief; in four or five days we were at work again, but we had learned a lesson not to be forgotten in a day. After this we touched it lightly and with gloves on. We heard of some cases where the eyesight was nearly ruined and the person's health was never reestablished again. Ivy and dogwood are pleasant to take, side of poison oak.

By the first of July we had the upper half of the island worked out, and Charles and George wanted to go down to Stockton to cele-

In Search of Gold

brate the Fourth. I said one must stay and I will be that one; so they hired two mules and started off the morning of the third and were gone a week, which cost them about seventy-five dollars. I kept the fourth by staying in the tent and reading, and I think I enjoyed myself as well, in the long run, as those that spent more money and felt worse the next day.

About a week after the boys came back, one morning just as I was getting up I heard a great racket in the hen house. I ran out as soon as I could, and there, about six rods up towards the gulch, our white rooster was hanging over the shoulder of a large red fox making for the mountain as fast as his load would permit. We let on all the steam we had and took after him, and at first we seemed to gain on him. As he was crossing the gulch and along the flat between the gulch and mountain, some eighty rods, we got so near that I yelled at him thinking he might drop the rooster, but no, he kept on. I don't think he was five rods from me when he began to ascend the mountain. I made a fresh spirt, but I was blown, and he went up the mountain two feet to my one. The boys were nearly up with me when I stopped, they ran on a short distance, and then seeing he had the lead of us, came to a halt. How provoking it was to stand and see that fox carry off that white rooster, the pride of "Six-Bit Gulch." It was Sunday morning but we did not swear; no, we seldom did, but we felt just like this, if we had had a gun we would have shot him; well we might have missed him after all. Well, we came back feeling sad but wiser men. We fastened the fowls in at night and let them out in the morning.

One night a short time after this, I was awakened by having some one put his hand into my pocket. I made a grab at the fellow and caught him by the sleeve and held on until I was drawn nearly out of the berth, when I had to let go. The fellow ran out and I after him. There was an oak log a few steps from the door, and not remembering it to be there in my excitement over it I went, falling heavily. If the scamp had known of my mishap he might have come back and robbed me then after all. Charles and George knew nothing of it until I came in and called them up to light a torch and look for tracks, which we did, and found it was a Mexican greaser by his

Chapter XVI

green hide boots. I was so badly hurt in my fall that I lost a day's work.

Our door was but a strip of hanging canvas and one could come in easy enough. We now cut some large oak logs and rolled them up for the sides and set some posts in the ground and then hung a door, made of oak splits, and every night when all were in we hung on the door a tin pan and a piece of iron; if the door was opened the pan would give warning. Indian squaws came round sometimes when we were out at work, and would steal anything they could lay their hands upon, so we fastened an old pan up over the test and then fastened a stone at the end of a rope, placing it over a pulley and down to the door. When the door opened the stone would strike the pan and make quite a loud noise. This was George's idea, and he was so pleased with the working of it that he kept up the racket for some time longer than was necessary.

The next day we went up to Chinese Camp to see them puddle. This is a new process to dissolve stiff clay. A large round cistern some six feet high and eight feet in diameter is used; the inside has an arrangement that is worked by horsepower that keeps the dirt stirred up in a plenty of water, the dissolved dirt floating out as new material is put in, the dirt paying about ten dollars to the man employed. The dirt is taken to the machine in one-horse carts, often from quite a distance. This place was discovered by Chinese, but were soon driven away.

They have made this place the county seat for the present, and here is held high court, a mockery in most cases. Lynch law seems to work the best of anything that has been tried. It settles the trouble for all time, and there is no chance for some future governor to pardon the miscreant and let him again prey upon the unwary.

Wood's Creek is on the other side of Chinese Camp and has paid well. In some places it has proved very rich, taking out three and sometimes four ounces a day to a man. At one place a man by the name of Sanderson took a prospect from quite a deep hole he had dug, striking the bedrock where there was what is called a pocket, a small hole in the ledge. This he found full of gold and clay, mixed about half and half, and out of that small hole he took seven thou-

In Search of Gold

sand three hundred and forty six dollars. He took it all out into a single pan and it was not quite full at that. That was a big strike and caused quite an excitement, and men went to digging with new ardor; this man dug his claim all over, but did not get fifty dollars more.

Thirty-two miles from here is a place called "Poverty Flat," where a man that had been working since 1849 and had made nothing, and at this time owed a week's board, and they would trust him no longer, went up above the camp about a mile and went down into a hole that was considered worked out. He had not dug more than a few moments when he struck something hard; it did not seem like a rock but gave a duller sound; he finally dug around it and after a good deal of prying he managed to get it to the surface. He scraped off the clay that was adhering to it and found it was very smooth, something in the shape of an egg; he dug around a spell longer and found a smaller piece, and this was all he could find. He now went down to camp and into the board house and said, "Will you give me some breakfast now?" His breakfast was brought on instanter, for the sight of the gold worked wonders. After getting his breakfast his mind began to dwell on his golden lumps, and before night he had become a raving maniac. The largest lump was worth a little over five thousand dollars, and the other three hundred dollars. He was taken to the insane hospital at 'Frisco, where he died a short time after. So you will see there is as much danger in getting too much as there is in not getting enough.

October had come and the days were getting cooler, and we could work more hours. We continued to work our island and the west side until the first of January, when the claim would not pay any longer, and a company of Chinamen came along, and after two days we managed to sell out to them for the sum of four hundred dollars, reserving, however, a small angle that we intended to prospect more thorough than we had done.

CHAPTER XVII

The Chinese — Sell Out and Leave the Mines — The Stage Driver Again — Stockton — Arrive at San Francisco — Start for Home — Virgin Bay — Virgin Lake — The San Joaquin River — The Rapids — The Steamer Northern Light — Setting a Deadhead Ashore — Arrive in New York — Take a Bath — Scenes and Incidents in the City — Etc., Etc., Etc.

There were over seventy Chinamen that we had sold out to; they are great workers, that is, they do not work so fast but keep constantly at it, living on rice and fish mostly. We used to go and see them eat with their chop sticks, and they did not seem to have any trouble in taking up their soups and fluids of any kind. They are very harmless too, letting almost any one drive them from pillar to post. The authorized collector would come once a week to collect their tax and others came as often as they dared to. We used to go and see them smoke opium; the way they do this, all sit down on the ground in a circle, the pipe is loaded, then each takes a whiff, and it is passed around until all are unconscious, except one or two left as guards; their faces have the appearance of death. They seem to have

In Search of Gold

a large number of holidays, using their firecrackers very lively; once or twice a month they were at it.

We sold our claim to seventy of them and had a good opportunity to observe their actions. One Sunday I tried to learn their head man a few words of English, and he tried to learn me to count one hundred; it sounded very odd; but it was entirely wrong to let those heathens come into the country and carry out the gold in such quantities.

The two brothers, Charles and George, after we had sold out, went down on the Tuolumne River to prospect, and were gone nearly two weeks, but could find nothing that would pay; in fact the most of the surface diggings were worked out, or down to two or three dollars a day, leaving but little after paying board.

About the middle of February I said to George one morning, "I think I will start next Monday morning." When that stage driver came along they were very much surprised at my sudden disclosure. I said I had been thinking it over for some time that if I started now I should arrive in season to commence market gardening in the spring; the cattle would not be fit for beef for a month, so I offered to sell my interest for so much and they bought me out; they intended to start home by the first of April, for they thought they had seen enough of California and its roughs. I was very certain I had. Shaw, who had kept the stagehouse, had gone two months ago, so the next Monday morning early, I rolled up my buffalo robe once more. It was now over two years that I had lugged it over my shoulder. We had sat up late the night before, talking over matters and things, but they were up to see me off, and as we shook hands George said, "I wish I was going too," and turned and went behind the tent; it was more than he could stand.

I could now hear the stage rattling over the distant hills on its way down to the stage house where the horses were changed, so I hurried down and across "Six-Bit Gulch" just as the stage came rattling up. Nothing must do but I should get up and ride down to the stage house, only a quarter of a mile distant, for he had heard I was going to start for the States. This was the same driver that was going to give us a horse whipping a year and a half before. The driver said,

Chapter XVII

"Aren't you going to have some breakfast?" I said I had eaten mine some time ago. "That won't do; you must have some with me, and it shan't cost you anything;" so after breakfast we started for Stockton, sixty miles distant, going over nearly the same route I had tramped on when I came up; quite a change had taken place since then; the land most of the way had been taken up for agricultural purposes and was quite largely fenced with wire, the "Lone Tent" had been replaced by a substantial farmhouse, and wheat and barley were looking nicely. I saw a few market gardens, but none for any great extent. But the city, how it had grown! It had spread out in all directions! I inquired for Dan, but none had ever seen him; old Uncle John's place had been crowded out of existence and I tried to find the hardware store and its owner, but could not; all had been changed; so I went on board the "Firefly" by night, a small steamboat running twice a week between Stockton and 'Frisco, two hundred miles.

The steamer left the wharf at five and arrived at San Francisco about five the next day. There had been a great change since I had been here in 1850; long wharves and piers had been built out into the bay, and large warehouses now stood where the New Jersey had dropped her anchors in forty-nine. Who could believe so much could be accomplished in so short a time? Where was the sand hill that looked so bare and desolate, and the well I went down into, hogshead over hogshead, for two hundred feet, to get a pail of water to mix some mortar? The hill was now covered with fine residences and the well had been filled up no doubt, for the water was as salt almost as the ocean, and on the other hill a railroad was being built. All the smaller rum holes and gambling saloons had had their day, and were the things that had been; there were plenty of gaming houses, but they were on a grand scale of magnificence, and not so much powder used as there once was in these hells upon earth.

I went into an office and bought a through ticket by the way of Nicaragua, paying three hundred and fifty dollars. This was paying out money by the wholesale.

There was quite an excitement here the day before we sailed. Adams' Express Co. had closed their doors and the bankers, Page,

In Search of Gold

Bacon & Co., were in some trouble. They said there had not been so many silk hats on the street for some time. We heard that a miner had made a deposit of five thousand dollars with Adams' Express Co. the day before their doors were closed, and intended to have gone home at the same time that I did. There were a great many stories afloat at this time. A story was started that three two-horse loads of specie had been taken from Adams' bank during the night, and some were for breaking down the doors and ascertain what had been done with the capital of the bank.

The next morning the Uncle Sam was to leave her wharf at ten o'clock for San Juan del Sud. She had about fifty passengers, mostly miners, returning to New York. The steamer Uncle Sam was a fine vessel of three thousand tons burden, almost new, and her officers were gentlemen and treated their passengers with great kindness; the weather was all that could be wished and the run was made in ten days. The ship was anchored in Virgin Bay, an enclosed sheet of water containing some six acres, more or less. We arrived at about ten and were taken ashore in a lighter; here was an American house for the entertainment of any that might want a dinner.

From here to Virgin Lake is eight miles over a macadamized road; at one o'clock, carriages drawn by four mules were provided for the passengers, each carriage holding eight, the native drivers cracking up their teams at a great rate; this was a splendid ride of eight miles. I think I never enjoyed a ride so much before.

All around the landing of the Lake soldiers were stationed to prevent the passengers from going down to a small village hard by; quite a number had been murdered there heretofore, among the Senoritas. The soldiers were obliged to prick some of them to keep them back. I don't think near so many would have thought of going if there had not been any soldiers, for this made them think there was something they had ought to see anyhow, and so they broke through the cordon, and when the roll was called to come on board to cross the Lake, two were missing.

The time had arrived for crossing the Lake, some fifty miles, I think. This was as fine a sheet of water as any one could wish to see.

The next morning at daylight we entered the river San Joaquin.

Chapter XVII

We now changed over into a larger steamer that was waiting for us here. The river is about three hundred yards wide, with but little current, a dense forest in full leaf coming up to the very edge of the stream and overhanging its dark, still waters. We could hear the song of many birds, and I could hear other noises too in the depth of the tangled forest.

In the afternoon we made another change into a smaller steamer. There was a general sameness all the way down the river, and not an opening did I see in all that distance; one continuous evergreen forest met the eye everywhere. We came to the Rapids, about four hundred feet long, and very steep; the roar of the waters over the rocks sounded like distant thunder. Just before we came to the Rapids the passengers were landed and met the boat below the Rapids, and it was an exciting scene to see that little steamer navigated among those rocks, they seemed to look at her pitching down that roaring cataract as though she must strike. We stood and trembled for her safety, but she came down with all the baggage without a scratch.

We now went on board again; here the country opens out again and the forest recedes. At evening time we were at tidewater, where we remained until the next morning, when we steamed out to the steamer Northern Light and drew alongside, and the officer took our tickets as we passed on board. There was a man that had no ticket. I saw him climb on board when the officers were not looking, and I thought I would see how he got on. When the passengers were all on board they were sent aft. They had discovered they had two more passengers than tickets; they found them after awhile and set them to work; one would work and the other would not, and they told him what they would do if he did not work, but he was determined not to conform to their wish.

There was another steamer anchored near by and they had a band of music on board, and as our steamer raised her anchor the band struck up "America," it sounded very nice as the sound floated over the water, their anchor was raised at the same time. Now came the trial of speed, and it was soon apparent that the Northern Light was the fastest boat by all odds, and by noon the Western was

In Search of Gold

out of sight.

About the middle of the afternoon of the third day we came in sight of an island, and when they had come within a mile they gave the man his choice, he could work or be set on shore; he said he would not work and so the vessel came to a stand, a boat was lowered and the man was taken to the island, a few provisions left with him, and the boat returned and was hoisted on board and the steamer moved on her away.

Nothing of any great interest occurred on the passage to New York, making the passage from San Francisco to New York in twenty-one days. I and a man by the name of Lamson kept together in travelling around New York City. The first thing we did was to hire a room for one day, and for this we paid one dollar. We started out on our voyage of discovery that we might purchase a new suit of clothes. We went up Broadway and into a large clothing store and were fitted out from head to foot. This cost us fifty-three dollars each, as we agreed to take two entire suits, and thus obtained them somewhat cheaper than we could a single suit, and as we wanted about the same kind of garments it worked well enough.

We now started out to take a bath and clean off the lice that had become our close and active companions; these we wished to shake off at the earliest opportunity. With these intentions we started down Water street, with many a reminder on our perforated skins that we were not alone by any means. On turning a street a thief jerked Lamson's bundle out of his hand and took to his heels. I was on ahead, and as he came by me I stuck out my foot and tripped him up. I got the bundle, and Lamson jumped on to the fellow and held him there. A policeman came along and took him in charge, and nothing must do but we must go up to the police room and make our complaint. What a nuisance dishonest people are when one is in a hurry!

After stating the facts in the case, we soon arrived at a bath house and went in. I asked the man what he would give for our clothes we had on, as we should put on new ones. He said, the price of the baths. I said it was a bargain on my part, and Lamson said he could have his. We gave ourselves a good cleaning up; we found our scalps

Chapter XVII

were all honeycombed with lice, but with plenty of soap and bay rum they were obliged to leave their covered ways and come out to the light of honest day. When we came out of that bathhouse we left it inhabited by millions! Shall I ever forget the Northern Light that contributed so much to our bodily discomfort?

We now walked around the city; what a great hurry every one seemed to be in! Lamson said they appeared to be going for the doctor. The noise made by the trains over the paved highways reminded me of the San Joaquin rapids.

As we came down Broadway two men got to fighting in the middle of the street; they had not made more than one or two passes at each other when a fire engine came along on a dead run and ran over both, killing one and knocking the other senseless. This attracted but little attention, as such things happened here almost every day.

CHAPTER XVIII

Start for Boston — Meet Shaw on the Steamer — Arrive in Boston — "Must have Gold" — Leave for Chicago — The False Lover and his Punishment — Visit the Farm House — The Entertainment — The Departure — A Scene on the Train — Leave the Train — In Search Of Lodgings — Etc., Etc., Etc.

As the hour was drawing near when we must go on the steamer Dean Swift, that left her wharf at five o'clock for Fall River, we went along the river front to view the forest of masts that one could see for a long distance. What a busy scene! Men going in all directions, each having an interest of his own.

We then went on board, and almost the first man I met was Shaw that kept the stage house on "Six-Bit Gulch." He was boatswain on the steamer Dean Swift. He was very glad to see me once more, took my buffalo robe, giving me a check for the same, and said it would be just as safe as though I took it into my stateroom. This robe had been my constant companion, and I did not wish to lose it. He said he had a good berth, the work was light and good pay, fifty dollars a month.

Chapter XVIII

Lamson and I took a state room at one dollar each. Shaw said he would call us before we got into Fall River, which he did, going around with a gong that made noise enough to raise a bushel of potatoes.

We arrived at Fall River about midnight where a train of cars were waiting to convey us to Boston. On board of these we went, and in a few moments they were off for the city that never sleeps, where we arrived about nine.

The next morning Lamson wanted I should go with him to the bank to get his money; he had a check on Wells, Fargo & Co. We found the bank and they asked what denomination he wished; he said, "Don't know; but I gave gold dust and I want gold for the check." They told him it would be heavy and bungling to carry and that bills would be much better for him. No, he must have gold. So they got a shot bag and filled it almost full of twenty dollar gold pieces. He was now satisfied and went down the outside steps swinging the bag in his hand. I said, "Put that bag under your coat; the prowlers will spot you and you will lose it." At the corner of the next street I left him, and whether he lost his gold or not I cannot say, but he was one of the kind that the sharps like to come across to their rounds after flats.

After stopping in the city a few days I bought a second class ticket for twelve dollars to Chicago. I thought I would save twelve dollars, and the agent said I should go nearly as quick. I was now starting for my western home, the grand prairie. The train left Boston at six the next morning, and the next night, at twelve, we changed cars at Rutland, VT.

So far, I had come first-class; this was getting on nicely. In about two hours the conductor came round to punch tickets, and when he took mine he said, "This is a second-class ticket; you must get off at the next station." "Very well," I said. There were some more young fellows on the same car, and they were very urgent that I should not get off, but an old gentleman said I had better get off, as in the morning I would have to get off and wait for the emigrant train anyhow; so at the next station the train was stopped for me to get off. This was nothing but a flag station, about the size of a smoke house,

In Search of Gold

not another house or barn in sight. About two in the morning, (this was cold work standing around here) they said the emigrant train would come along about nine in the morning, so I thought I might as well be going along to the next station.

In about three miles I came to quite a village, but they were all abed and asleep for anything I knew; not a light could I find. I had said over to myself more than a dozen times, "Well, this is a pretty fix," when I observed a head peering at me from behind a small house and soon another from behind a house further along. I thought, what is going on here; I went to see if the first head had a body, and when I had got within some thirty feet he came out and wanted to know who I was and what I wanted. I said I had been left by a train some three miles back and had started on in hopes of finding some place open that I might get some rest. "Well," he says, and here the other man joined him, "you stay here awhile with us and then you shall go up to our house and stop."

He then went on to tell me after we had moved behind the house that a man had jilted his sister and was now paying court to another down at yonder house and they wanted to catch him and learn him a lesson he would not soon forget. I said, "Aren't he sitting up rather late?" They said it was after this time that he went home last week, but they had missed him in the gloaming or fog. We continued to talk for a half hour longer when I spotted a man coming from the house they had mentioned. "That's him," they both said; so when he had got as near as he would in passing that way, they both walked out to him. I could see he was about to take to his heels, but thought better of it. I could see, too, that one of the others was about to take hold of him, for they were having some hard words between them, when this fellow, I will call him Bill, gave the tallest brother a tremendous blow side of the head, sending him on to the ground in a hurry; he then went for the other one, but he met him and they clinched, Bill coming uppermost. Now came the tug of war; the other one was sitting up and rubbing his head, wondering what was the matter. I had come up close to them, but not intending to interfere; the brother underneath had Bill by the throat and Bill with one hand was trying to draw a knife. I then thought it was

Chapter XVIII

time for me to interfere. I said, "Let go that knife," but he would not, and in spite of all the other could do nearly succeeded, and would if I had not worked in a blow that convinced him the battle was up. I was willing that they should give him a good trouncing, but nothing more. The first brother had come to understand the situation and Bill sitting up rubbing his head, the youngest brother now gave Bill a good pounding, and I thought if the sister had been here she would have said, "That will do." I now said, "Not another blow;" they then got up and made Bill promise to leave the place by sunrise that morning or they would not answer for his life. I thought what a pity it was that he who could handle himself so well should be so mean in his love affairs.

The brothers now invited me to accompany them home; day was just breaking in the east as we arrived at the farm house where they lived. There seemed to be no other farm houses in sight and it seemed to be in rather a lonely place, some two miles or more from the station, on a flat and wet plain, with not a tree or bush to rest the eye upon.

As I stood taking a survey of the country the brothers had gone in and had struck a light; they then asked me to come in, which I did, and presently the old folks joined us and I was duly introduced to them, giving them the particulars of the morning's striking exhibition. Soon the boys went out to milk and do their morning's work. They had five yoke of oxen, seven cows, eight horses and several colts; some of the latter they were breaking to harness; they also had eighty-five Southdown sheep and they had a very fine place. They considered this part of their industry the most profitable of any, as the wool was always in demand and sold for cash.

When we came in to breakfast I was introduced to the daughter; she came forward and took my hand and said she was glad to meet one who had assisted at the punishment of him who had treated her most shamefully. She was glad to see me at her father's house, and she would endeavor to make my stay as pleasant as possible. I should be considered as one of her brothers and should call me brother James. This was a good beginning certainly; could I ask more, certainly not. She was well dressed and quite good looking, and about

In Search of Gold

twenty years of age.

We sat down to breakfast, and a good one it was too; this looked very home-like. I looked towards the daughter to find her eyes fastened on me. During our meal they asked me of my travels in other lands, and were very much interested in the accounts I gave them. They urged me to stop over until the morrow; my ticket was good for a month, they said, and why couldn't I stay and go a hunting and fishing; they would go with me to the Great Falls, they would try their best to entertain me if I would only stay, but no, I could not; I must go on to my farm in the West, it was my fate, my destiny perhaps. I thanked them sincerely for their hospitality and pleasure, and hoped to meet them again, perhaps on my return if I did not find things as I could wish.

The hour for my train was drawing near and I said I must be going; not yet, if I must go I should ride to the station. The hour had come, the team was at the door, and now we must part. The girl gave me a look of gentle reproach as much to say, "Why will you go!" and after we arrived at the station I was strongly tempted to return with them, but destiny was stronger than will and I must follow its lead.

The train soon came in sight and stopped at the station. I then bid the two brothers goodbye and went on board. Here was a mess and no mistake; foreigners mostly, and largely from the Emerald Isle, four coaches crowded to their full capacity; they were different from any others I had ever seen; the windows were small and nearly at the top of the car, and it was almost impossible to see out unless standing up; a single bench around the sides in order to make most of them stand up, the same as on the cattle cars; each family had from five to twelve children, all the way from the size of a pin to a pork barrel, of all colors and descriptions that ever was known on land and water. If I had known what a place it was I could not have been hired for love or money; the cars were the same as so many night carts; they made no stops to accommodate the passengers and they only stopped to get wood and water. A few times they went on sidings for a short time to let trains pass. These night carts were hitched on to a freight train and therefore moved at a snail's pace,

Chapter XVIII

and it seemed as though we were suffering for all the sins we had ever committed, or ever might, let them be ever so bad.

There were two American families, the mother and her two daughters sat opposite to an old gentleman and his daughter. I sat next to the front end of the car, so that we Americans were together and kept that end somewhat decent. The old gentleman and I—I will call him Foster—Foster and I talked a great deal; his daughter was a nice girl and could converse on all topics of the day. She said her father wanted to visit his son-in-law living in Illinois, and he being rather feeble she came to take care of him. I found before we got through I had to take care of them both. What long days and nights those were! I could leave my seat only at night time, the same with Foster and his daughter, for some of the brutes would get them in our absence.

The fourth day, at ten o'clock at night, the train came to a stop in the company's freight yard. I asked Foster if he intended to stop in the cars until morning or go to some lodging; the girl said we are entire strangers in this city and father is so very feeble, so I must call upon you to see us out of this difficulty, and she said it with such trusting sweetness I could do no less than say I would do the best I could for them; her eyes spoke volumes of thanks.

The first thing was to find our way out of this labyrinth of freight cars, for they seemed to cover acres of ground. After a long tramp under, over and around, we reached the open street. It was nearly eleven o'clock and all places of business had been closed long before; we found none open except hotels and saloons of doubtful character. I went into the hotels and inquired their price for lodging while they stood in the street. In some they charged two dollars, others one dollar and fifty, others a dollar. The old gentleman said he could not pay over a dollar. The girl told me to use my own judgment. Where they charged a dollar they did not look any too honest. One place I went into and when I came out not having been gone more than five minutes, I found them gone; who could have spirited them away so soon. I looked up and down the street but could see nothing of them. I went up the street until I met a policeman. I inquired of him but he said he had seen no such parties. I then started back again, thinking perhaps they had gone the other way, and as I was crossing a street I saw them coming down; the girl was glad enough to see me. She said I had not been in the hotel three moments when a man came along and asked them what they were looking for. Her father said lodgings. He said "Follow me, I have a house close by very cheap and nice." She said her father would go after him all she could do, and she had to go with him that he might not be lost or robbed. When they went into the place she saw at once it was a low place, and she told her father she should not stay there if he did; this decided him to come away. She said the man went to the door and was going to stop them from coming out. She told him to stand out of the way or she would call the police. He then stepped aside and they came out. I said that was a narrow escape; I began to feel anxious as to your whereabouts, but am glad it is no worse.

I now charged the old gentleman not to leave me until I had found them a suitable place to lodge, and he promised not to leave me again. The girl was entirely worn out and she said, "How can I thank you for all this trouble?" I said I was trying to find a place for myself as well.

We continued to travel nearly a half hour longer when I saw a sign, "American House, Board and Lodging." The door was fastened and I knocked and a man opened it directly and asked what we wanted. I said a night's lodging. He said, "How came it you are out so late?" I told him and he said it was very late and he was about as full as he had ought to be, but would try and stow us away somewhere; "And you, young man, will have to go up garret." "Very well," I said, "I shall be rising in the world." Now I said, "What will you charge us for lodging and tomorrow's board? It being Saturday we must stop over until Monday morning." He said, "Fifty cents for lodging and a dollar a day each for board." I said, "You can have our custom until Monday morning." He said, "If you had been three moments later I should have been in bed." He now showed the father and daughter to their rooms and then came back and we began to ascend until we reached the roof. In the attic we found a cot bed. "There," he says, "is the last unoccupied bed in the house;

Chapter XVIII

it is not much, but perhaps you can make it do." I said, "I had not had any sleep for four nights that had done me any good, and I should be sound asleep before he reached the basement." Sleep, nature's sweet restorer. I slept with a clear conscience, disturbed only by dreams of emigrant trains and their unpleasant associations.

CHAPTER XIX

A Kindly Greeting — Illinois — The Population — Leave for the "Grand Prairie" — Arrive at Kankakee City — Meet "Sam" — The Disappointment — Return to Chicago — The Farmer's Exchange — The Letter — Start for Webster Creek — Sickness and Death of "Alice" — Arrive in New York — Home Again — The End.

When I awoke the next morning the sun was high in the heavens and I felt refreshed. Sleep had done wonders; it had cleared away all previous bad impressions that had centered around my heart for the last few days, and as I went into breakfast Miss Foster came forward with a kindly greeting that had a large amount of sunshine in it. She hoped I had rested well and my dreams had been pleasant ones. I thanked her for her kind solicitude and hoped her rest had not been broken by unpleasant dreams connected with the late emigrant train as mine had been. The old gentleman wanted to know if I couldn't go with them out to his son-in-law's, on Webster Creek, some fifty-five miles; nothing would please him better if I would go and it should cost me nothing, and his son and daughter would try to make my stay pleasant and agreeable. I looked towards

Chapter XIX

the daughter to see if she would second the motion; she looked at me but said nothing; perhaps some other young man dwelt in her memory.

After breakfast I took a walk around the city of planked highways, viewed the rising walls of the Illinois Central Depot, built of stone. The city has spread out in all directions since I was here last, and there seems to be a large floating population here at this time. The foreign emigrants meet here and then spread out over all the lands in the great West, and still there is room for more. The Germans are the most tidy and best farmers by all odds, and they understand how to economize in every particular; the most wealthy farmer in all the West is a German.

The next morning at breakfast I again met the old gentleman and his daughter Alice. During our conversation I said in an hour I should be on my way to the Grand Prairie, and perhaps we should not meet again. Alice looked up with a sweet smile and said she hoped our acquaintance, so favorably commenced, would not be so suddenly terminated. She had got rested now and was more like herself again and could better understand and appreciate my disinterested kind services. She said her father had given me an invitation to join them at her brother-in-law's home, and if I could make it convenient she hoped I would not disappoint them. I thanked her for the kind offer, but it would depend largely how I found my affairs on my arrival at my destination.

I then bid them goodbye, with my best wishes, and I hurried to the depot and purchased a ticket for Kankakee City, nine miles to the South of our farm. Sam was standing on the depot promenade and I came up behind and gave him a good slap on the back that made him turn around as though he had been on a pivot. This was a joyful meeting after a three years' absence. "Well, Sam," I said, "How is everything since I have been gone?" "Well," he says, "I am afraid you will feel disappointed at what has taken place since you have been gone. In the first place, you know, I was to look after the place, and when it came into the market I was to purchase the same, and in the event of its being one of the odd sections belonging to the railroad company, I was to purchase it on the best terms I could.

Well it did prove to be one of those sections that the road claimed, and they would not sell it for less than ten dollars an acre, and not having the necessary funds at my command at the time, I could not make the purchase and it has steadily been rising in value. I have rented the place for the first two years to a man by the name of Hanscom for a certain sum, but after a time it became evident that he was a worthless scamp and I tried to oust him; the result was the house was burned and the insurance having run out some two months previous, it has become a total loss; the fencing material I sold at a fair price; the improvements can be sold for something, but not a great deal." I said, "Give me a certain sum and I will exchange receipts." He was in company with another man at this time and had sadly neglected my interests; he agreed to do this and we tied up our affairs in this way. I now took care of him in a friendly way and started for Chicago, where I arrived the next morning.

I went to the Farmer's Exchange, the place we had put up at three days before, and when I went in the landlord was glad to see me. He said the old gentleman and daughter had left a letter there for me in case I should return that way, and as she knew not my address she thought it better to leave the letter with him. He then handed it to me and I read the following words: "Soon after you left us I was taken quite unwell and I fear I am going to be sick; if you should see this would you be so kind as to come out to Webster Creek, for I fear for my poor old father." The landlord looking over my shoulder, said, "You will go of course?" "Yes, I thought I would;" and so I took the next train for Webster Creek, where I arrived at two in the afternoon.

I soon found Foster's son-in-law's place. The old gentleman was out walking and was very glad to see me. He said his daughter Alice was quite sick; she had taken the emigrant fever, and I must go in; she would be glad to see me. Just then his son-in-law came up and I was introduced to him. We came in where the daughter was sitting in an arm chair, looking very pale. She was glad to see me and was glad I had come. I said I had got her letter and came on directly and I hoped she was not seriously ill, but was sorry to see her look so pale. She said she had contracted the disease on that emigrant train.

Chapter XIX

We talked some time longer and then I went out to look over the place with the son. The farm lies on both sides of the Creek, high rolling prairie, well adapted to the growing of all kinds of grain. Their most profitable investment was cattle raising, of which they had some three hundred out on the ranch, grazing.

The next day Alice was much worse; so they were obliged to call in the local doctor. He said she would be around again in a few days, but instead grew rapidly worse. I was about to take my leave when the old gentleman called me in and said Alice wished to see me. I followed him into the sick room and was greatly surprised to see how fast the disease had done its work. She called me up to her and said, taking my hand in hers, "My life is nearly at an end." I said, "No, I hope not." She was young and I hoped she would yet recover. At the same time I could see that the great destroyer had marked her for his own. She had called me because she had formed a good opinion of me and knew she could trust her poor old father in my care, and that I would see him to his distant home and leave him in the care of mother. She broke down entirely, after a while she went on—"I and mother had talked this journey over for more than a year; how much father and I have looked forward to the enjoyment of this visit, of the incidents upon the way, the different people we should see, and all those things new that a constant changing brings into view; but alas, our mode of travel was anything but pleasant, except the little sunshine that came into my life for a few short days." I said, "Let that green spot remain in your heart while it continues to beat." She smiled faintly and lay back on her pillow, and during the night she grew rapidly worse and at the dawn of a new day she went to her rest. I stopped until after the funeral wishing to return to New York.

I said to the old gentleman, "We will start for home tomorrow morning bright and early." He seemed dazed by his bereavement and it was some time before I could make him understand that he was to return home. The next morning we bid our friends goodbye and started on our return to New York, taking first-class tickets, where we arrived the third day. Here I delivered the old gentleman to his wife and friends; my promise had been fulfilled. After stopping with them until the next morning, giving them the events as they had transpired, and wishing them all happiness, I left for Boston, where I arrived the next morning. In my search for gold I found it pure and unsullied from the hand of the Creator, and now having travelled by land and water forty-one thousand miles, I feel that I shall roam no more, but settle down to constant labor, adding my mite to the support of the millions.

The End

The Cranberry Webb Worm

Not a sound was heard but the bluebird's note
    As down to the meadow we went;
And we saw by the vines the worms had come,
    On their annual mischief bent.

Slowly, but surely we laid them out,
    Paris green from our engine flying,
And we saw by next morning's early light
    The enemy was surely dying.

Few and silent were the words we said,
    And we spoke not one word of sorrow;
But with pleasure we viewed the millions of dead
    And cheerfully planned the morrow.

No useless covering incased our hands,
    For we knew we had work to perform;
To kill and destroy some millions of worms
    And carry forward the needed reform.

There's a tide in the affairs of men;
    There's a turn in the tide of the worms,
And now we look encouragingly forward
    To next autumn's fair returns.

Appendix — John Fisk's Lineage

Possibly the earliest ancestor in the Fisk family has currently been traced back before 1066. In the Phillimore edition of the Domesday Book for Norfolk (section 34,20 under the lands of Peter of Valognes), a free man named Fish is entered for Wood Dalling, in the Hundred of Eynsford. (Source: *www.fiske.clara.net/*).

The following is a list of the direct ancestors of John Fisk. The first three, Daniel, Hugh an Hugh are only probable, and they have been discovered as a result of research since Frederick Clifton Pierce's *Fiske and Fisk Family* genealogy compiled in 1896.

Daniel Fisc — From *Fiske Family Papers* by Henry ffiske, 1901. Daniel Fisc's name is appended to land grant issued by King John in 1208.

Hugh — Born about 1340, of Hoxne, County Suffolk and Laxfield. Said to be a probable descendant of Daniel Fisc.

Hugh — Born about 1370 in Laxfield, England. He was probably either the son or grandson of Hugh above. Mentioned in charters of 1421 and 1435.

Appendix — John Fisk's Lineage

Lord Symond Fiske — Born about 1399, died 1463; res. Laxfield. His will is dated Dec. 22, 1463. Symond is the earliest Fiske listed in the Pierce genealogy. (Pierce 1)
William Fiske— Born 1420-1425. Of Studhaugh. Died about 1504; res. Laxfield. (Pierce 2)
Simon Fiske — 1462-1538; res. Laxfield. (Pierce 10)
Simon Fiske — Died 1505; res. Laxfield. (Pierce 28)
Robert Fiske — About 1525-1623; res. St. James, South Elmham, and Ditchingham, Norfolk, England. (Pierce 58)
Jeffrey Fiske — Died 1628; res. Metfield, England. (Pierce 83)
David Fiske — 1601-1660; res. Watertown, MA. (Pierce 134)
Lieut.David Fiske, Esq. — 1624 (England)-1710; res. Watertown. (Pierce 172)
David Fiske— 1650-1729; res. Lexington, MA. (Pierce 199)
Dr. Robert Fiske — 1681 or 1689-1753; res. Lexington. (Pierce 294)
David Fiske— 1737-1815; res. Lexington. (Pierce 444)
David Fiske— 1760-1820; res. Lexington. (Pierce 743)
Jonathan Fiske — 1786-1871; res. Lexington. (Pierce 1318)
John Fisk — 1829-1905; res. Billerica, MA. (Pierce 2535)

In the Pierce genealogy, John is the first listing of his lineage to not include the 'e' at the end of Fiske. In my research, I encountered a number of disparities between various sources, such as whether Lord Symond was known as Simon and had claim to the title "Lord" at all. Most of these are posted on the internet without real documentation and are the highly questionable opinions of amateur historians. This purpose of this appendix is to correct a few details in the Pierce record as well as present accepted theory established since 1896 regarding the earliest Fisks.

John Fisk descends as well from Thomas Rogers, who was born in England in 1571 and arrived in Plymouth on the Mayflower in 1620. Fisk's wife, Judith DeCrow descends from William White, who was born in England in 1591 and also was a Mayflower passenger.

ABOUT THE EDITOR

Bruce Adam was born in Chicago. He studied at Lake Forest College and Harvard before graduating from Northern Illinois University with honors. He then moved to Nantes, France where he taught and continued his studies. Returning to the US, he worked ten years in publishing before turning his attention to completing his own work. He has published three volumes of short stories with Ara Pacis: *Dreams of a Lifetime*, *The Voyage of a Bean*, and *Zen Death Poems and Other Stories*.

www.ingramcontent.com/pod-product-compliance
Ingram Content Group UK Ltd.
Pitfield, Milton Keynes, MK11 3LW, UK
UKHW041418180426
11947UKWH00007B/191